REVISIONING PENTECOSTAL ETHICS –
THE EPICLETIC COMMUNITY

REVISIONING PENTECOSTAL ETHICS –
THE EPICLETIC COMMUNITY

Daniel Castelo

CPT Press
Cleveland, Tennessee

Revisioning Pentecostal Ethics – The Epicletic Community

Published by CPT Press
900 Walker ST NE
Cleveland, TN 37311
USA
email: cptpress@pentecostaltheology.org
websites: www.cptpress.com
            www.pentecostaltheology.org

Library of Congress Control Number: 2012943425

ISBN-10: 1935931288
ISBN-13: 9781935931287

For Cornelio and Annette Castelo

TABLE OF CONTENTS

ACKNOWLEDGEMENTS

This work stems from a concern that Pentecostalism, particularly in its North American context, has changed over the decades in ways that have at times been inconsonant with the movement's instantiating ethos. Of course, all inquiry of retrieval and reconstruction happen from a particular vantage point, and mine, as limited as it is, can be prone to generalization, romanticism, and pessimism. Nevertheless, the present work seeks to continue a conversation, one that I have sustained with others about where the movement has been and where the subtradition could be headed.

The prominent influences for this project have been my teachers and mentors. Of these, the two most formative have been my parents, Cornelio and Annette Castelo. Because of their lives and ministries, I have been given the gift to see Pentecostalism through a number of lenses and contexts. These include different regions and countries as well as varying levels of denominational hierarchy. I dedicate this work to them out of gratitude for what they have meant to me and what they have managed to offer to God's kingdom through their lives of sacrificial service.

Additionally, two groups of people merit mentioning. The faculty of the Pentecostal Theological Seminary has played a pivotal role in my formation as a believer and scholar. They nursed me in theological education and pushed me to fly once they saw I was able. They encouraged me to pursue doctoral studies and allowed me to test arguments and ideas with them, both in the classroom and (more importantly) in private conversation. Although I owe them all for their impact upon my life, I mention particularly those who sustained important dialogue with me during my formative seminary years: Jackie and Cheryl Johns, Steven Land, John Christopher Thomas, Rickie Moore, Kim Alexander, Lee Roy Martin, Doug Slocumb, French Arrington, F.J. May, James Beaty, Hollis Gause, and Oliver McMahan. My appreciation for this community will forever be genuine and profuse.

Finally, I had a number of formative teachers at Duke University, and I thank all of them for their time and energy spent on my behalf; the one who has been most available and supportive of me is Stanley Hauerwas. His influence is quite detectable throughout this work. With the exceptions of Grant Wacker and his students, Stanley usually knew more about me and my theological tradition than any other person in a given room of Duke faculty and students, and his knowledge was based on sources other than my own testimony. For his interest in and support of my life and career, I am most grateful. I know he has meant a great deal to many, many people, but I wanted to say publicly that he has been a gift to me. Thank you, Stanley. As I have told you many times before, I have tried to be faithful with what I have learned under your tutelage. This work is but one more expression of my debt.

I have enjoyed discussing these topics with a number of people. My colleagues at Seattle Pacific University, particularly Rob Wall, are always supportive of my work. Kate Bowler proved to be an enjoyable sounding board for the project. Chris Thomas and Lee Roy Martin were supportive of this project early, and I wish to thank them for bringing it to print through CPT Press. And of course, my immediate interlocutors, my wife Kimberly and our daughter Kathryn, have been constant reminders of both the possibility and necessity of embodying one's commitments.

In terms of sources and venues associated with the research in this volume, Chapters 2 and 3 are significant expansions of an early article: 'Tarrying on the Lord: Affections, Virtues and Theological Ethics in Pentecostal Perspective', *Journal of Pentecostal Theology* 13.1 (2004), pp. 31-56. Chapter 4 originated as a paper delivered at the conference 'Toward a Pentecostal Ecclesiology: Implications of the Five-fold Gospel – Constructive Theological Proposals' held at Bangor University, Wales in June 2010; the paper was later published as 'The Improvisational Quality of Ecclesial Holiness', in John Christopher Thomas (ed.), *Toward a Pentecostal Ecclesiology: The Church and the Fivefold Gospel* (Cleveland, TN: CPT Press, 2010), pp. 87-104. Finally, Chapter 5 is a modified version of the chapter 'Patience as a Theological Virtue: A Challenge to Pentecostal Eschatology', in Peter Althouse and Robby Waddell (eds.), *Perspectives in*

Pentecostal Eschatologies: World without End (Eugene, OR: Pickwick, 2010), pp. 232-46. My thanks to the publishers and editors of these venues and collections for permission to use portions of this material in what follows. Scripture quotations contained herein (unless otherwise noted) are from the New Revised Standard Version of the Bible, copyright 1989, by the Division of Christian Education of the National Council of the Churches of Christ in the USA. Used by permission. All rights reserved.

My hope is that this work will be of benefit to God's people as they strive to be faithful to God and one another.

dc
Advent 2011
Ahuachapán, El Salvador

INTRODUCTION

What follows is a constructive exploration of moral theology within Pentecostalism. As such, a few words are in order by way of circumscribing, justifying, and setting forth the task at hand.

1. Preliminaries

First of all, the focus of this work is on American Pentecostalism, particularly its classical and trinitarian forms. Sometimes, I generally speak of 'Pentecostalism' or 'Pentecostals', but when I do, the particular referent is to this specific orbit, one tied to the Azusa Street Revival of 1906 and manifest in the early denominations that came about shortly before and after that event. Such delimitations are not meant to imply that the heart of Pentecostalism is properly reducible to this time period and location; plenty of counter-evidence could be offered to make such privileging moot. Also, I suspect much of what is on offer in this volume could be generalizable to other Pentecostal and broadly Christian contexts since it is a proposal that attempts to take seriously the pneumatological underpinnings and possibilities of an enacted and embodied moral theology. Nevertheless, such a vision, if it is to do 'work', has to be located 'somewhere', and in this sense, I find it especially helpful to be as particular as possible as an entryway for any potentially generalizable momentum. I leave the thrust and possibilities of generalizing these proposals to others who are more aware of the variety of contexts in which Pentecostalism thrives today.

As a constructive work, the following monograph seeks to build off of the important historical investigations on offer by the most capable interpreters of early Pentecostalism; it does so, however, without the aim of rivaling their work. The present endeavor assumes certain readings from historical inquiry so as to move to theological construction. Some may not find the assumptions I employ compelling given their readings of the historical evidence, but that is the nature of the constructive task: In such endeavoring, some things are assumed in order to move the discussion forward. For instance, I continue to privilege the early years of the American Pentecostal Movement, but I do so not out of a romantic impulse, one that esteems early Pentecostalism in this context as more pristine than contemporary iterations; rather, I privilege this period in part as a way of garnering 'institutional memory' regarding the movement's trajectory so as to establish a basis by which to evaluate historical and theological continuity and divergence. As I will repeat throughout this work, I believe that early Pentecostals harbored certain impulses and intuitions that were quite important but that over time were diminished or reconfigured in light of a number of pressures that arose over time. Such capitulations are not necessarily conclusively nor are they irretrievably corrupting, for the movement has continued in a spirit both consonant and dissonant to what has preceded it. In other words, I am suggesting that in my constructive negotiation of materials I do not find early Pentecostalism to have had it 'always right' nor do I suffer illusions that its contemporary iterations have it 'totally wrong'.

2. General Outlook

Of course, the rub largely rests on what is meant by 'it', and for my purposes, the referent is to a normative vision for what the 'epicletic community' looks like. The expression requires some elaboration. I have chosen to focus on a 'communal' rather than an 'individualist' framework since much of this work is striving to take stock of the Pentecostal Movement throughout its history, one that I intentionally label as a 'subtradition' of the church catholic. As counterintuitive as it may seem on first blush, Pentecostalism ought to engage in reflection that understands itself ecclesially more so than revivalistically since specifically within the American context revivalist fires have waned over the years and the revivalist model itself is increasingly being particularized. Altar experiences, as helpful and as continually necessary as they are, cannot carry the sheer weight of forming a sustainable witness over time. A collective ethos has to be attended to, and this process involves both retrieval and envisioning. The second feature of the phrase, namely 'epicletic', is a doxological as well as pneumatic term.[1] The word usually is associated with the eucharistic prayer as a way of preparing the elements for their partaking by the faithful. This preparation involves 'calling' the Holy Spirit 'upon' the elements and communicants alike. This activity is illustrative of how the church is to be in its coming and going in relation to God, one another, and all else that is. It is a fellowship that lives its common life with the ongoing recognition that its life is Spirit-offered, Spirit-dependent, Spirit-enlivened, and Spirit-empowered. An epicletic community then is one that is disposed and characterized in a certain God-like and God-directed way. As Yves Congar titles the last section of his major work on the Holy Spirit, the life of the church is 'as one long epiclesis'.[2]

Within these doxological, ecclesial, and pneumatic inflections, I offer what I term two 'practice-orientations' that can illustrate the epicletic nature of Christian communal life, and these are 'abiding' and 'waiting'. Within these two practice-orientations can be subsumed a number of particular practices, affections, and virtues. Part of their appeal rests on the fact that they are themes found in Scripture as indicative of the disciples' and church's calling within the present order. As practice-orientations, abiding and waiting are largely synergistically indeterminate: they involve God's prevenient work but also human response and activity, all in ways that are often unclear and indefinable to curious humans who want to know 'who is doing what'. Such a quality is helpful so as to position both the active and pathic dimensions of the Christian life in a mutually enlivening manner rather than in an arrangement where a myopic

---

[1] I have previously used the language of 'tarrying' to denote much of what I aim to do with 'epicletic' since both terms are doxological in nature. The advantage of 'tarrying' is that it is a term employed by Pentecostals to speak of the existential phenomenon I hope to consider extensively in this monograph; its difficulty (and ultimately what led me to choose another term) is that it continues to promote revivalist impulses (the altar encounter, the individual seeker, and so forth). Again, revivalist impulses are not wrong, but one argument I wish to stress is that Pentecostalism involves much more than revivalist fires; they overlap, no doubt, but they are not synonymous or coextensive terms.

[2] Yves Congar, *I Believe in the Holy Spirit* (3 vols.; New York: Crossroad Herder, 2000), III, pp. 267-74.

privileging of a certain side of the divine-human encounter takes place. When these extremes are ventured (when the change or activity is labeled either as 'all God' or 'all human'), they often result in unhelpful categorizations and agent-related overdeterminations. It is important to note that throughout any account of moral theology, God is the primordial agent, initiator, and sustainer, and yet we as God's creatures are involved in important and unique ways. Our participation is not so much a threat to God as it is indicative of God's hospitality, gratuity, and love.

3. Why Moral Theology?

Early American Pentecostals were driven by a restorationist impulse, and I am of the persuasion that, a naiveté of simply reconstructing the first-century church notwithstanding, the intuition is earnest and justifiable in a certain sense, not simply on hermeneutical grounds but theological ones as well. In this light, I think Grant Wacker has captured the root of this restorationist passion quite compellingly:

> Stepping back in time, quietly slipping in early pentecostals' kitchens and parlors, I heard, first of all, a great deal of talk about Holy Ghost baptism. I heard how God's Spirit entered their bodies, took control of their tongues, and gave advice on life's most mundane decisions. I also heard about the Bible, its power, its beauty, and the way it served as the final authority on all questions of daily living as well as human salvation. And I heard about signs and wonders – drunkards delivered, eyes restored, unlettered folk speaking foreign languages they had never studied. The more I listened to those discussions, however, the more I realized that most of them were really about something else. And that something else, of course, was God ... typically [the desire to touch God] suggested a yearning simply to know the divine mind and will as directly and as purely as possible, without distorting refractions of human volition, traditions, or speculations.[3]

---

[3] Grant Wacker, *Heaven Below: Early Pentecostals and American Culture* (Cambridge: Harvard University Press, 2001), p. 11.

In my opinion, the sensibility that Wacker points to is largely constitutive of Pentecostalism's *theological charm*. How can one deny the beauty, humor, and sheer delight of seeing people yearning simply to know God in a more profound way? This charm is one of the reasons, I believe, that those of us who were raised in Pentecostal environments cannot shake their effects, even as much as sometimes we would like to do so because of pressures and excesses one can readily sense. The matter is not just about being true to oneself and one's history as an embedded, particular being; it also relates to the simple fact that often Pentecostals are some of the most passionate people after God one encounters in one's lifetime, and given the love commandments in Scripture, those that are said to be the chief summary of the law and the primary way by which we are to relate to God and everything else, something about such passion just seems right.

In this light, given the way the vision of God inflects everything for Pentecostals, I have found it appropriate to pursue the Pentecostal ethical task under the rubric of *moral theology*. Some may not understand or be compelled by this move, but I find it to be crucial. Oftentimes, moral theology is associated more with Roman Catholicism than Protestantism, and I believe that differentiation partially rests on Protestantism's dependence upon and perpetuation of certain modernist claims and assumptions, especially as they relate to the natural-supernatural divide, the rise of the viability of something denominated as 'secular' or 'universal' reason, and the reduction of human beings to individualistic 'thinking things'. The fact that Roman Catholicism has continued 1) to raise the possibility of exorcisms and other rites and traditions that assume the existence of a supernatural realm, 2) to foster (however successfully) a mystical tradition alongside its scholasticizing impulses, and 3) to consider human and divine action as interplaying synergistically in important ways all contribute to the conclusion (no doubt troubling for many) that Pentecostalism and Roman Catholicism have some strong affinities. Of course, Protestantism occasionally shares some of these impulses as well (for instance, as evidenced in this study, through the Wesleyan and Holiness Movements), but the oft-detectable divergences between Pentecostalism and certain sectors of Protestantism make the former something importantly distinguishable from the latter and so correlationally alignable in significant ways to those traditions that have resisted some of the more damaging effects of modernity within Western culture.

These ruminations matter for the task at hand because Pentecostals have tended to operate from the intuition that the vision of God and the vision of human flourishing are closely tied; the former sets up the possibilities and limits for the latter. Such a tendency is best portrayed or on offer within ethical investigation through the language of moral theology. For this reason, the present work seeks to mine this field of inquiry and its methodological presuppositions as a way of constructing and offering the ethical task within Pentecostalism through a framework that is amenable to the ethos of Pentecostalism as a whole. By such a choice, I am not suggesting that endeavoring that emphasizes 'social ethics' or other forms of moral inquiry cannot be important for the movement, but I find such work to be insufficiently methodologically attentive to the theological impulses and rationales that have traditionally driven and shaped Pentecostal life. For Pentecostals, the presence and action of God within doxological space and mode change and alter everything, including whatever one decides to say about something as awkwardly and counter-intuitively denominated as 'Pentecostal ethics'. Given the Pentecostal ethos, I believe that such a task has to be framed within the integrationist conventions and sensibilities that the field of moral theology displays, for moral theology audaciously suggests that the way one goes about living in the world ('moral') is unquestionably and determinatively shaped by one's vision and participation in God ('theology').

4. The Structure of the Book

The book will proceed in the following way. Chapter 1 will offer a programmatic account of certain features of Pentecostal identity as a way of securing the legitimacy and propriety of moral theology within the Pentecostal fold. Chapters 2 and 3 will survey two significant models that are especially helpful for a Pentecostal moral theology, namely the affections and virtues, respectively. Pentecostals have pursued treatments of what constitutes normative affectivity in the Christian life, and these will be surveyed alongside a thorough reception of the Wesleyan account of such matters so as to depict in a more directed way what can constitute a normative account of Christian affectivity within Pentecostal theological-ethical inquiry. Virtue theory, on the contrary, has not been pursued significantly by Pentecostals, but it represents another model that especially attends to the 'from below' aspect of kingdom living. Both the affections and virtues will be employed as frameworks by which to concretize conceptually the dialectic of 'abiding' and 'waiting'. Finally, Chapters 4 and 5 aim to show the need for Pentecostal moral theology by highlighting two major theological-ethical features of its embodiment that are currently in disrepair. These two issues are the vision and pursuit of holiness amidst pressures for and against codification as well as the non/viable shape of eschatological expectancy. Both chapters, then, will offer critique and reparative reconstruction in light of the dynamic of 'abiding' and 'waiting' on display within the conceptual frameworks of the affections and virtues. The goal in both cases is a salutary reconfiguration of what it means to inhabit the Pentecostal ethos as a doxological and pneumatic existential; in other words, the vision is of and for the epicletic community.

1

PENTECOSTAL BEING-IN-THE-WORLD

Ethical inquiry within the Pentecostal academy has recently started to receive the attention it has long deserved, but for many years it was a neglected feature of Pentecostal theological endeavoring. Such a state of affairs has been lamentable since the progression from reflection to enactment was a quick one among early Pentecostals, making Pentecostal embodiment both generative and precarious for theological and ethical negotiation. Unquestionably, Pentecostals have been prone to consider embodiment to be part and parcel to theological relevance and legitimacy. The acts of 'testing the spirits' and supporting a person's ministry if the person is deemed to be 'anointed' have led to a number of developments that have been controversial and distinctive, including the recognition of women, ethnic minorities, and even children as capable of participating in ministerial capacities. Therefore, the validation of a person's fittingness for ministry (broadly speaking, since lay and clergy distinctions have tended to be very fluid in Pentecostalism's underdeveloped forms) has traditionally been undertaken through the attestation of a person's spiritual integrity, one that is instantiated by the power of God upon a person's life and sustained through the practice of the spiritual disciplines in an ongoing and constant way. Therefore, most Pentecostals would agree with the impulses on display in James McClendon's systematic trilogy: The first step in assessing the Christian faith has to be an embodied life.[1] Faith-

---

[1] James McClendon's approach continues to be unique; the volume in question is *Ethics: Systematic Theology*, volume 1 (Nashville: Abingdon, 1986).

fulness in performance is a gateway for being affirmed as a person of theological and spiritual authority. One must begin, then, with ethics.

The transformative encounter that shatters and reconstitutes Pentecostal believers is often dramatic. Undeniably, some with time return to their old ways after these moments, but others experience a significant turnaround, one implied by the language of *metanoia*. If one assesses Pentecostal testimonies, especially those of yore in the American context and contemporary ones from around the globe, the nature of the transformation and its related outcomes often bridges the gap between spirituality and ethics. Some are slain in the Spirit *and* others are delivered from substance abuse; some speak in tongues, *and* others stop beating their spouses. The act of being encountered by God is assumed to have the potential for changing people 'from the inside out' so that they truly have a new identity, becoming in the process 'new creatures in Christ'. The process is not automatic or universal, but Pentecostals have always been marked by a certain expectancy that something out of the ordinary could happen as a result of God's encounter with humanity at the 'altar moment', that instance when God 'shows up'. That expectancy no doubt has been fueled by antecedents that have spurred the imagination.

Some critics, however, have lamented what they see as a one-sided approach to Pentecostal approaches to ethical matters, claiming that American Pentecostals in particular have been neglectful, indifferent, and maybe even antagonistic toward social justice and other societal and systemic concerns. One of the assumptions often held by these interlocutors is that an overemphasis on the spiritual (meaning that the cause of all evil is understood to be at its root a spiritual problem) has led Pentecostals to neglect a feature of their responsibility toward the wider world. If real change is said to happen at the altar, what about the many evils that plague both society and the church in a more systemic way? Why, these observers persist, have Pentecostals not been more active in ameliorating society's ills?

One such critic is Robert Mapes Anderson, who argued in his classic study that Pentecostalism's forebears, those in the Holiness Movement of the nineteenth century, were more interested in 'social welfare' than 'social reform', as indicated by their relative conservatism in relation to social change. This conservatism, which is in Anderson's mind an antitype to revolutionary tendencies, emerges out of a sensibility that would assume that 'too great an emphasis on social reform could undermine the "spirituality" of the faithful and divert the Church from its central task'.[2] According to this reading, Holiness folks and their ilk generally were of the opinion that 'individual regeneration was the chief means of social reform' and that the latter would happen naturally by the conversion of the masses through those called to such ministry.[3] He remarks: 'The independent Holiness people saw the source of social problems in fallen human nature, which found expression in the social order through individual men. The solution was clear: men must be saved and sanctified, that is, morally regenerated as individuals'.[4] This reading moves to consider Pentecostalism as emerging out of this capitulation implicit in Holiness conservatism, and in turn, Pentecostalism became even more isolated and disillusioned with political processes as a result. Pentecostals were, to use Wacker's way of phrasing Anderson's estimation, 'three-time losers' in that they were victims of status disinheritance, economic plight, and cultural despair, leading them to hate or check-out of the social system.[5]

Wacker's more recent study is not so overtly bound by Anderson's ideological commitments, but the conclusions he draws are nevertheless similarly bleak. Through his poles of the 'primitive' and the 'pragmatic', Wacker attends to the common life of early American Pentecostals in order that he may show the tensions between what they said about themselves and what they actually did. In terms of Pentecostal social involvement, particularly in relation to the state, Wacker remarks, 'The main factor [for pentecostals'

---

[2] Robert Mapes Anderson, *Vision of the Disinherited: The Making of American Pentecostalism* (Oxford: Oxford University Press, 1979), p. 196.

[3] Anderson, *Vision of the Disinherited*, p. 196. According to Anderson, Pentecostalism arose in America because of frustrations held by its early pioneers with regard to their class struggles. Their inability to address the sources of their frustration led them to misdirect their energies toward internal strife, thereby resulting in a conservative approach to social reform. This reading, of course, is a form of the deprivation theory; for recent treatments of this theory in relation to Pentecostal origins, see the essays by Peter Althouse and Adam Stewart in Michael Wilkinson and Steven M. Studebaker (eds.), *A Liberating Spirit: Pentecostals and Social Action in North America* (Eugene: Pickwick, 2010).

[4] Anderson, *Vision of the Disinherited*, p. 198.

[5] Wacker's thoughts on Anderson's work can be found in his review of Anderson, *Vision of the Disinherited* in *Pneuma* 4 (1982), pp. 53-62.

disengagement from the political realm] was principle, and principle decreed that governance of the state simply fell outside the Christian's proper sphere of concern … Men and women who felt they had little stake in America or its future simply had no time to worry about the affairs of Caesar'.[6] And so, the idea that 'the church ought to support political measures to alleviate physical suffering … found little resonance in pentecostal circles'.[7]

Wacker's reading, however, points to something truer about Pentecostal motives than what comes across in Anderson's reductive and ideological narration. If one takes Wacker's analysis into account, the Pentecostal rationale for political disengagement would not be strict apathy or misplaced frustration relating to anomie; rather, it stemmed significantly from a theological consciousness, one that pivots on what could be termed a 'church-world' typology. Within this understanding, the principalities and powers of this world order are fallen, an assumption that in turn shapes subsequent involvement (or lack thereof) within political processes.[8] In relation to early American Pentecostal approaches to the state, Wacker's remarks are telling: 'Holy Ghost folk were never very analytical about these matters. But they meant at least this: Christians' fundamental allegiance should never be lodged with the state since the state was an earthly fabrication'.[9]

Some observers like Anderson would find such reactions as sociologically explainable in terms of class struggle, and undoubtedly, the legitimacy of this reading must at least be permissible to some degree; however, at play in Wacker's assessment, at least explicitly and on the surface level, are theological claims, and these should be

---

[6] Wacker, *Heaven Below*, p. 223.

[7] Wacker, *Heaven Below*, p. 223.

[8] It should be noted, however, that this kind of political 'noninvolvement' is nevertheless a species of testimony to the state and the wider public because it is a 'stand' or 'posture' of sorts. In refusing to be 'politically active', Pentecostals were nevertheless being controversially political. As John Howard Yoder, *Discipleship as Political Responsibility* (Scottdale: Herald, 2003), p. 44, remarked, 'We will remember, along with the New Testament church, that one form of political responsibility is to refuse, under certain circumstances, to participate in the life of the state, namely in those situations where the state oversteps the boundaries of its mandate, as in totalitarianism, and in those situations where the state's responsibilities differ from those of the Christian, as in the military'. A more sustained treatment of the matter can be found in John Howard Yoder, *The Christian Witness to the State* (Eugene: Wipf and Stock, 1998).

[9] Wacker, *Heaven Below*, p. 217.

taken just as seriously in subsequent analysis since these are explicitly how Pentecostals have traditionally justified their behavior.[10] In other words, Pentecostals have often formulated *theological* warrants (however nascent and inchoate in form) for their approach to the wider society. Therefore, theological methodologies of evaluation, alongside other disciplinary approaches, ought to be used in negotiating this outlook and stance by Pentecostals. Social-scientific and other disciplinary methodologies should not be privileged over theological ones simply because they are assumed to be 'less subjective and biased' by the academic establishment. Once Pentecostal approaches to the wider world are considered on their own terms (that is, theologically), one can come to recognize the existence of something that could be termed Pentecostalism's 'critical tradition'.

1. Pentecostals as Critically Astute?

Like their Holiness counterparts beforehand, Pentecostals have traditionally been marked by a peculiar species of eccentricity,[11] a kind that led Walter Hollenweger to say that a 'critical tradition' has been operative in Pentecostalism from its earliest manifestations in American Pentecostalism and in more up-and-coming Pentecostal contexts throughout the world today.[12] These saints have 'taken stances' on matters that were not simply related to privatized religiosity (like the charismata) but also ones very much tied to the public presence of the gospel in key matters related to political, economic, and cultural arrangements.[13] These commitments have been

---

[10] This tension makes Anderson's book very difficult in terms of its subsequent reception by Pentecostals. Its ethnographic rigor was unparalleled at the time of its writing, and such findings and elaborations were deeply helpful; its ideological commitments, however, were reductive and off-putting, given their totalizing explanatory presumption.

[11] I draw this language from Douglas M. Strong, 'Sanctified Eccentricity: Continuing Relevance of the Nineteenth-Century Holiness Paradigm', *Wesleyan Theological Journal* 35 (2000), pp. 9-21.

[12] Walter J. Hollenweger, 'The Critical Tradition of Pentecostalism', *Journal of Pentecostal Theology* 1 (1992), pp. 7-17.

[13] To take but one example, Stephen Prothero's survey of the world's religions remarks quite favorably of the way Pentecostalism has been active on the public scene throughout the world (see Stephen Prothero, *God is Not One: The Eight Rival Religions that Run the World* [New York: HarperOne, 2010], pp. 87-91). For a fuller treatment of global Pentecostalism and its 'progressive' forms, see Donald E. Miller and Tetsunao Yamamori, *Global Pentecostalism: The New Face of*

internally contested and tenuous, and their advocacy has often been inconsistent and mixed, but one of the common features surrounding this Pentecostal testimony has been precisely its form: *Pentecostal advocacy has largely been in terms of confession and testimony.* The way Pentecostals have 'taken stances' on issues of social concern has usually been through their attempt to shape, deepen, and stay true to their convictions in their own lives and as these relate to everything else. Such negotiation is inevitably a very public matter (especially if it involves being 'out of step with the times').

Along with desegregated meetings early on, perhaps the most telling example of this eccentricity is the early pacifist persuasion of many first and second generation Pentecostals. Early American Pentecostals were significantly pacifistic because of their restorationist roots that in turn led them to a particular reading of the New Testament, especially one focused on themes related to the life of Jesus and the nature of the kingdom he ushered.[14] Yes, eventually an accommodation on this topic did occur among many denominations, but at least up to the time of the First World War, Pentecostals were taking controversial stances on war and military service and were doing so on the basis of explicitly biblical and theological warrants,[15] ones that were rooted in a communal ethos informed by a particular consciousness.[16] These believers participated in a specific way of seeing and reading the times that in turn allowed them to

---

Christian Social Engagement (Berkeley: University of California Press, 2007); for a more theologically constructive account, see Amos Yong, *In the Days of Caesar: Pentecostalism and Political Theology* (Grand Rapids: Eerdmans, 2010).

[14] See Joel Shuman, 'Pentecost and the End of Patriotism: A Call for the Restoration of Pacifism among Pentecostal Christians', *Journal of Pentecostal Theology* 9 (1996), pp. 70-96; see also Jay Beaman, *Pentecostal Pacifism: The Origin, Development, and Rejection of Pacific Belief among the Pentecostals* (Hillsboro: Center for Mennonite Brethren Studies, 1989), and, most definitively, Paul Alexander, *Peace to War: Shifting Allegiances in the Assemblies of God* (Telford: Cascadia, 2009).

[15] Alexander notes that early Pentecostal 'adherents saw Jesus as central. They interpreted Scripture through Jesus' eyes; this meant that the Old Testament stories and arguments that seemed to contradict Jesus' teachings were not authoritative' (*Peace to War*, p. 31).

[16] Granted, these positions were *not deeply* rooted, for, as Yoder observed, Pentecostals did not believe in being deeply rooted (John Howard Yoder, *Christian Attitudes to War, Peace, and Revolution* [Grand Rapids: Brazos, 2009], p. 262). However, the peculiarity of Pentecostal positions on pacifism and race relations during the early years of the movement points to an impressionistic indeterminacy that was refreshingly counter-cultural despite its precariousness.

maintain their marginality (at least for a time and related to a few particular issues) because of their commonly shared convictions.

One key moment for this expression was the Assemblies of God resolution of 28 April 1917, twenty-two days after the USA declared war on Germany. Wacker's elaboration and quote here are helpful:

> The resolution began by noting that the Lord Himself had ordained human governments, and affirmed unswerving loyalty to the government of the United States. But it went on to state that the inspired Word of God, which served as the exclusive basis of faith and practice, instructed Christians to seek peace and not to shed blood. The critical concluding sentence of the resolution read: 'THEREFORE we, as a body of Christians, while purposing to fulfill all the obligations of loyal citizenship, are nevertheless constrained to declare we cannot conscientiously participate in war and armed resistance which involves the actual destruction of human life'. The resolution's immediate purpose was to qualify the sect as a pacifist denomination in the eyes of the government, thus allowing partisans to apply for noncombatant status along with Quakers, Mennonites, and other peace groups.[17]

As indicated by Wacker's last remark, early American Pentecostalism may have been similar to the Anabaptist traditions in that their negotiation of scriptural, christological, and pneumatological commitments created a nexus of eccentric possibilities that beckoned attention from an onlooking world because of its challenge to the status quo. What was missing, however, from the Pentecostal fold that has been forged and shaped over time among Anabaptists was the ecclesiological dimension; the shifts that rapidly ensued point to one theologically devastating lacuna: *The first and second generations of classical Pentecostalism did not have a sufficiently strident and robust ecclesiology so that they could sustain their countercultural witness over time.*[18] What is

---

[17] Wacker, *Heaven Below*, pp. 244-45, quoting the Resolution in the *Weekly Evangel* (4 August 1917), p. 6.

[18] This point is Yoder's (see Yoder, *Christian Attitudes to War, Peace, and Revolution*, p. 263). Yoder's comments are brief here regarding Pentecostalism and yet (in typically Yoderian fashion) straight to the point. He recognized that Pentecostals read the Bible and 'took it straight'. That is, I would imagine, a theological achievement in Yoder's mind, but it is not enough if by 'enough' one means that which would make possible a sustainable witness over time.

meant by 'ecclesiology' here, however, is not simply a perspective on the church; at greater stake at this point is a collective sense of identity, one that was sufficiently well-defined, perpetuated, and transmitted so that the tests of fellowship and the temptations toward accommodation could be overcome in a faithful, collectively supported, and intentionally extended way.[19] Precisely it is this ecclesial lacuna, no doubt exacerbated by Pentecostalism's mobility, transiency, and self-understanding as an 'outpouring' or eschatologically framed episode of redemptive climax and fullness, that led to astonishing and shameful fragmentation that blighted the movement so early in its American instantiations. And it is this ecclesial shortsightedness that continues to plague the movement even though it is now, at least in many of its classical and American forms, denominationally saturated and institutionally overdetermined.[20]

2. Assessing the Loss of Eccentricity

The existence of Pentecostal eccentricity (at least in its sanctified forms) points to something beyond an altar encounter. Although Pentecostals privileged this kind of experience through their practices, speech patterns, and expectations, their 'critical tradition' suggests that more has been at play in Pentecostal identity and life than simply individualized and emotionally charged experiences. Early Pentecostalism and subsequent embodiments of the movement have had the makings of a *way of being* in the world. To use alternative terms, Pentecostalism in its nascent and embryonically institutional stages implies a way or form of life that is potentially communally sustainable. Only within this kind of setting could such a

---

[19] This problem is much more complex than what can be treated here, but the complexity points to the difficulty of institutionally sustaining a mystical tradition, and this challenge has perplexed Christianity from the beginning. In narrating the matter in such a way, I am assuming that Pentecostalism is best understood as a mystical tradition within the church catholic, a claim that I hope to argue in another work.

[20] Within the Pentecostal academy, the topic of ecclesiology has recently become a matter of serious investigation; Dale Coulter, Simon Chan, Frank Macchia, Amos Yong, Veli-Matti Kärkkäinen, and others have significantly contributed to the discussion. The difficulty here is that such developments within the academy have not necessarily found corollaries within American denominational structures, faith statements, or deliberative mechanisms per se.

politically charged option like pacifism ever come to be. As Lisa Cahill has remarked,

> Pacifism ... does not begin so much as an ethical reply to the violence question ... but as a practical embodiment of a religious conversion experience – as a way of life rather than a theory. Christian pacifism is essentially a commitment to embody communally and historically the kingdom of God so fully that mercy, forgiveness, and compassion preclude the very contemplation of causing physical harm to another person.[21]

Early American Pentecostalism had the possibility of posing a witness that in turn could have had massive implications for the religious *and* secular establishment. The pneumatologically prompted intuitions in question, those garnered in doxological receptivity and enactment, could have been sustained as an ongoing, collective witness. And one senses that both the possibility and challenge of the task are on display and available with every subsequent instance of Pentecostal revivalist fervor. In other words, those intuitions, because they are pneumatologically prompted, continue to be available today, but their cultivation and perpetuation become increasingly difficult to sustain as the environments in which they are prompted become more and more staid and inflexible. It is no wonder then that Pentecostal historians have resorted to the language of 'waves' to differentiate charismatic renewal in the twentieth century (with each wave corresponding to a different ecclesial arrangement), for with time, institutionalization has a way of suppressing renewal.[22]

If these pneumatic impulses are to be sustained in a viable fashion over time, then Pentecostalism's persistent insistence to identify itself as primarily a movement needs to be reconfigured. One way

---

[21] Lisa Cahill, *Love Your Enemies* (Minneapolis: Fortress, 1994), p. 2, as quoted in Alexander, *Peace to War*, p. 32.

[22] The Weberian 'routinization of charisma' that Margaret Poloma speaks of in her work is apropos here (see for instance Margaret Poloma, *The Assemblies of God at the Crossroads: Charisma and Institutional Dilemmas* [Knoxville: University of Tennessee Press, 1989]). Obviously, hers is a sociological construct, but its force is phenomenologically profound. How do charisma and institutionalization co-inhabit and mutually inform and contribute to one another? In this regard, Catholic charismatics may have something to contribute to classical Pentecostal self-understanding since the former have this concern at the forefront of their identity negotiation. One thinks, for instance, of Yves Congar in this regard.

to do this kind of work is to locate the heart of Pentecostal identity beyond and more deeply within revivalist currents that are short-lived and fleeting. In other words, the need here is to identify those particularities and sensibilities that stem out of Pentecostal worship and revivalist fervor into the everyday lives of Pentecostal believers. What is required is a deeper sense of the Pentecostal way of life. One resource that can aid in this endeavor is James K.A. Smith's recent work *Thinking in Tongues*, which attempts to make a contribution to Christian philosophy from the Pentecostal-charismatic perspective. Smith has tried to capture the pentecostal ethos by way of the language of 'worldview'. In Smith's estimation, Pentecost is a kind of hermeneutic, a 'construal of the world, an implicit understanding that constitutes a "take" on things', including (and most especially, given the thematic of the present volume) 'a take on ... being-in-the-world'.[23]

Smith's choice to use the language of 'worldview' is certainly permissible as long as it does not become or is assumed to be overly technical and intellectualized, and he is aware of the point: Whereas the matter on the surface appears conceptually prohibitive, Smith makes it plain that worldviews in his understanding denote pretheoretical understandings and intuitions that are closer to confessions of faith than consciously chosen positions.[24] He draws from Martin Heidegger's distinction between objective/propositional 'knowledge' (*Wissen*) and inarticulate/intuitive 'understanding' (*Verstehen*),[25] Charles Taylor's notion of the 'social imaginary',[26] and Amos Yong's idea of the 'pneumatological imagination'[27] to make the point of how often humans simply 'feel their way around' in their existences, that their being-in-the-world is often a matter more of the heart and what they love than an issue of the mind and what

---

[23] James K.A. Smith, *Thinking in Tongues: Pentecostal Contributions to Christian Philosophy* (Grand Rapids: Eerdmans, 2010), p. 25.

[24] Smith also deals with such qualifications in James K.A. Smith, *Desiring the Kingdom: Worship, Worldview, and Cultural Formation* (Grand Rapids: Baker Academic, 2009), pp. 63-71.

[25] The sections in question are §§31-32 of Heidegger, *Being and Time*.

[26] Charles Taylor, *Modern Social Imaginaries* (Durham: Duke University Press, 2004), particularly chapter 2.

[27] Amos Yong, *Spirit-Word-Community: Theological Hermeneutics in Trinitarian Perspective* (Eugene: Wipf and Stock, 2002), chapter 4. Also at play for Smith and this present monograph is the language of 'way' or 'form of life', phrases often associated with Ludwig Wittgenstein.

they think. If such is the case broadly with human beings and more specifically with people's faith commitments, then certainly it is true with regard to movements like Pentecostalism. The enactment and sustainability of faith commitments and convictions rest on commonly shared and perpetuated intuitions, ones that are enacted and passed on through collective practices.

Smith raises five possibilities that he believes would inform a Pentecostal worldview,[28] and whereas these elements certainly are viable, the broader challenge when speaking of a 'pentecostal worldview' is precisely its tacit character. The difficulty of this worldview remaining in the 'background', and so potentially suffering from cognitive underdevelopment, is that a conscious and sustained effort of identification, negotiation, and discrimination has usually not taken place within sectors of the movement as time has taken its toll, thereby leading to a self-inflicted blindness by adherents in terms of knowing how to sustain their identity in a manner faithful to its initial impulses and how to discriminate what influences or practices could deter, hamper, or even corrupt it all the while rapid growth and cultural assimilation take place. To recall the example of early Pentecostal pacifism, the matter over time shifted from being a biblically justifiable practice given the form of Jesus' life to a privatized affair related to one's individual conscience. The transition, as harmless as it appears on first blush, was theologically devastating. Why the shift itself, and why this particular gesture toward the individual's conscience? One can speculate that part of the issue at play included that this alternative was more generalizable to a constituency that was changing not only in terms of its numbers and make-up but also in its relation to the wider world. The shift appears to be one in the direction of modernist epistemological assumptions as well as populist tendencies. Simply put, the movement became more culturally mainstream, and with such a move, early American Pentecostalism strove to become more like its Evangelical counterparts, a tendency that would only further envelop it (once again, tacitly) within assumptions related to epistemology,

---

[28] These include '1) a position of radical openness to God, and in particular, God doing something differently or new; 2) an "enchanted" theology of creation and culture; 3) a nondualistic affirmation of embodiment and materiality; 4) an affective, narrative epistemology; and 5) an eschatological orientation to mission and justice' (Smith, *Thinking in Tongues*, pp. 32-33).

hermeneutics, anthropology, and other disciplines that contribute (either productively or deleteriously) to theological identity and self-understanding.

The danger, of course, with exercises of institutional memory and retrieval is to romanticize the past and to consider the present pejoratively. When one recognizes how the movement was born in controversy as well as tended ever so quickly to become fractious and divisive on doctrinal, racial, and other factors, one is hard pressed to memorialize a 'golden age'. And yet, traditions (like their adherents) are constantly evolving and changing, and at regular intervals that change has to be evaluated in terms of the originating circumstances and ideals of the tradition itself. The process, when undertaken in an intentional and earnest way, is salutary and mandatory for any tradition that wishes to perdure in a coherent manner over time. The concern registered at present is that these efforts have rarely taken place within the classical Pentecostal fold, and when they have, they usually have tended to be both defensive and reactionary, thereby leading to the crystallization of doctrinal and practical minutiae, ones that de-emphasize Pentecostalism as a form of life and affirm it simply as another Evangelical group (and all of the modernist entrapments that come along with that designation in the American context) with certain pneumatic accoutrements. With the center of American Pentecostal identity fundamentally changing, the tradition has not carried on favorably with the passing of generations. Of course, exceptions always exist to the rule, but the epicenter of Pentecostal vitality, much like Christianity as a whole, has shifted elsewhere than the American scene. Pentecostals in the trans-Atlantic world have become just as susceptible to the Western religious malaise as their older and more established Christian counterparts, developments that perhaps suggest that accommodation has won the day over sanctified eccentricity.

3. Claiming a Distinct Identity

Is there a way forward in the midst of this morass, and if so, what would such a recourse look like? Those within the Pentecostal academy have pressed forward with some important observations and proposals. These devoted scholars have given of their intellectual energies to assess and evaluate the tradition that they dearly love for the purpose of healing and repairing it as an act of faithfulness to God so as 'to hand over' (*traducere*) what they have witnessed to subsequent generations. Particularly in the American context, the work and travail of the scholars associated with the Society for Pentecostal Studies have represented important strides in terms of identifying and evaluating what constitutes the Pentecostal ethos. Their sustained deliberation, oftentimes undertaken in the face of denominational marginalization, has uncovered and narrated features of the Pentecostal way of life that are worth retrieving and extending. Some of these achievements are noted in what follows.

First, classical Pentecostalism within America would do well to continue to distinguish itself from American Evangelicalism, for the latter represents a number of sensibilities that are not commensurate with the Pentecostal ethos. Naturally, one of the significant issues here relates to scriptural interpretation. Pentecostals and Evangelicals (especially of the fundamentalist variety) in America generally have different 'canons within the canon' (Luke and Paul, respectively), and they secure biblical authority in varied ways (a pneumatically guided *lectio divina* compared to a propositionalist sufficiency that tends to inerrancy). But the issues run deeper still. If American Pentecostalism is broad enough to consider both Reformed and Wesleyan features of the nineteenth century Holiness Movement, then different anthropologies and hamartiologies could be involved as well.[29] Furthermore, given the way that Pentecostals largely have maintained a theological vision lacking in a robust distinction between the natural and supernatural realms, they have tended to resemble pre-modern epistemologies whereas Evangelicals continue to pursue truth and knowledge on largely modernist assumptions. No doubt, any number of pressures (including cultural, economic, and political ones) exist for Pentecostals and Evangelicals to assume they approach the Christian faith in significantly compatible ways; however, the ongoing capitulation to this pressure only has meant that Pentecostals have gradually lost the resources necessary to maintain their eccentricity, that which significantly makes them a valuable charism to the wider whole of Christianity.

---

[29] For a sustained adumbration of the issues on the Wesleyan-Pentecostal side of such issues, see Henry H. Knight, III (ed.), *From Aldersgate to Azusa Street: Wesleyan, Holiness, and Pentecostal Visions of the New Creation* (Eugene: Pickwick, 2010).

Second, as it has been assumed throughout this work, Pentecostalism generally is best understood as a spirituality that requires embodiment and performance for its logic to be on display and accessible.[30] The movement did not begin in a lecture hall, royal court, or ecclesial meeting but rather in the context of revival and worship. For this reason, Pentecostalism broadly is a doxological movement; its life is the context of worship. *Pentecostalism's way of being-in-the-world is epicletic in nature, meaning that it continually acknowledges that its source and end are made possible by the presence, prompting, and empowerment of the Holy Spirit.* Through the Pentecostal lens, life is lived continually *coram Deo* (before God) for all to see. For this reason, the integration of mind, heart, and body is deeply valued, and of all the constructs available to make sense of this integration and performance, the notion of spirituality is especially fitting.

4. Moral Theology rather than Christian Ethics

With such integration being vital to Pentecostal identity, the question of ethics then is not simply an add-on to a catalogue of theological modes of inquiry; rather, theological ethics is very much at the heart of Pentecostal life precisely because of their emphases upon embodiment and performance. To modify Stanley Hauerwas' famous phrasing of the church more broadly, Pentecostals traditionally have not had a social ethic; rather, they have been one.[31] Traditionally, to be integrated into the Pentecostal fold meant that in a very real and pressing way something drastic had to happen. In light of the severity of the occurrence, one's life was expected to be fundamentally altered and recalibrated accordingly.

If such reasoning holds, then the ethical question is not a separate or tangential matter to Pentecostalism; it must be configured and narrated in a very particular way, one that attends precisely to the Pentecostal ethos. If the center of Pentecostal identity and life is its epicletic existence, then the form of ethical enquiry most suitable for accounting and extending this way of life would be moral theol-

---

[30] The classic expression of this sensibility is Steven J. Land, *Pentecostal Spirituality: A Passion for the Kingdom* (JPTSup 1; Sheffield: Sheffield Academic Press, 1994).

[31] Stanley Hauerwas, *The Peaceable Kingdom: A Primer in Christian Ethics* (Notre Dame: University of Notre Dame Press, 1983), p. 99.

ogy rather than Christian ethics per se. Although the tendency by some may be to conflate these categories because they both attend to what people do, their differentiation is crucial for delineating a host of concerns associated with the manner and shape of moral inquiry within Christianity.

The distinction between the two categories rests on developments that have occurred in Western intellectual history, a history in which Christianity has had a place of privilege because of its Constantinian arrangements with the ruling powers and cultural elites. This course of events suggests that something dramatically occurred in the field of moral inquiry with the turn toward modernity, and the totalizing effects of this Copernican revolution are still widely felt today. Moral theology, a field often associated with pre-modern modes of moral reflection, operates from a vision of God and as such stems from and is directed to the church and its confession; it is 'integrally united with dogmatic and spiritual theology as the systematically ordered study of the journey of a human person, made in the image and likeness of God, back to the Father'.[32] As a theological discipline, moral theology stands alongside and dovetails with systematic or dogmatic theology. Both areas broadly are two sides of the same ultimate concern, namely how to behold and enact faithfully the holy mysteries graciously given by God to the people of God.

Christian ethics, on the other hand, aims to be a more public and universal category through its address of such 'modern social formations ... as the nation state, corporation, global market, or the university'.[33] The field tends to be promoted explicitly in terms of making decisions that relate to the Christian engagement with the wider world. Although generalizations are always difficult, Christian ethics often entertains the question 'What should we do?' more so than 'What kind of people are we trying to become?' With the focus on 'right action', a latent ambiguity surrounding the 'we' in question is repeatedly sustained.

---

[32] Romanus Cessario, *Introduction to Moral Theology* (Washington, DC: Catholic University of America Press, 2001), p. 1.
[33] D. Stephen Long, 'Moral Theology', in John Webster, Kathryn Tanner, and Iain Torrance (eds.), *The Oxford Handbook of Systematic Theology* (Oxford: Oxford University Press, 2007), p. 457.

This differentiation in categories and the preference often given to Christian ethics today largely stem from the assumption that 'doctrine divides whereas ethics unite'.[34] Of course, that assumption is empirically false,[35] yet it has a particularity all its own in which it is advanced and held to be tenable and right. The claim is just as 'biased' (and one could say, just as *doctrinal*) as other claims because operative in the suggestion of normatively framed activities such as 'dividing' and 'unifying' is an account of goodness, and all accounts of goodness require contexts to sustain and advance them. Because of its orientation and assumptions, Christian ethics is a relatively modern invention; there was a time in which it was not.[36]

Moral theology privileges the knowledge of God, one rooted in seeing and experiencing God, as a way of advancing in the knowledge of self and everything else that is. This kind of God-knowledge is not gnostic but very much tied to embodiment, performance, and conditionedness[37] because it draws from a vision of

---

[34] Long, 'Moral Theology', p. 458. The worry is that in tying moral judgments to doctrine, one would capitulate to a morality based on convention and so arbitrariness; the model would be too parochial for emerging modernist sensibilities. Therefore as a way of fending off moral relativism of this sort, a 'universal' basis was proffered by, among others, a Prussian philosopher of the eighteenth century who never in his lifetime strayed too far from his hometown of Königsberg.

[35] Interestingly, what often counts for 'hot-button' topics of debate, ones that are at the heart of the 'culture wars' within the American scene, are matters of moral contention. Alasdair MacIntyre's 'disquieting suggestion' continues to appeal in our contemporary setting as a helpful analogy for understanding the fractured nature of moral debate today (see Alasdair MacIntyre, *After Virtue* [Notre Dame: University of Notre Dame Press, 2nd edn, 1984], pp. 1-5). Nevertheless, operative within these debates is the shared expectation that a 'right answer' is available through reasoned argumentation, an expectation that makes moral inquiry deeply contestable and strife-laden in addition to nauseatingly interminable.

[36] Stanley Hauerwas, 'On Doctrine and Ethics', in Colin E. Gunton (ed.), *The Cambridge Companion to Christian Doctrine* (Cambridge: Cambridge University Press, 1997), p. 24; see also Stanley Hauerwas and Samuel Wells, 'Why Christian Ethics Was Invented', in *idem* (eds.), *The Blackwell Companion to Christian Ethics* (Oxford: Blackwell, 2006), p. 28.

[37] James J. Buckley and David S. Yeago, in their editors' introduction to the generative volume *Knowing the Triune God: The Work of the Spirit in the Practices of the Church* (Grand Rapids: Eerdmans, 2001), state that the central claim of their book is that 'knowing the triune God is inseparable from participating in a particular community and its practices – a participation which is the work of God's Holy Spirit' (p. 1). Given the alternatives for pursuing God-knowledge that have made their way in modernity, this particular approach avoids the pitfalls of a Hegelian synthesis and a gnostic propositionalism and in doing so makes doxological and epicletic ecclesial existence paramount.

God that is all-consuming and all-demanding.[38] As such, it involves liturgical practices, spaces, and modalities rather than a 'Kantian epistemology in an effort to secure relevance and consensus'.[39] All these features contribute to the assessment that Pentecostal ethics is best approached as a kind of moral theology. Given the way that Pentecostalism is a form of life that is existentially epicletic and doxological, any Pentecostal account of the good has to be grounded, shaped, and inflected by the presence and work of the triune God. It is from this source that Pentecostals can move to render accounts of the nature and task of being the community founded at Pentecost and empowered to live in the midst of the world through the power of the crucifixion and resurrection of Christ.

With these guiding orientations, one can sense the eschatological impulse, one that Pentecostals have repeatedly raised as the theological locus that best attends to their self-understanding in terms of identity and mission.[40] If a Pentecostal ethic is best framed in terms of a moral theology, one that envisions what the community of faith is called to be, then that teleological vision is eschatological through and through. If God is the beginning *and end* of all that is, then a vision of the moral life, when framed in Christian terms, has to attend not only to the interplay of creation, fall, and redemption, but to healing and beatitude as well.

---

[38] Another way of drawing the distinction further between the two fields outlined above is to say that moral theology begins with a vision of God's character whereas Christian ethics starts with the commanding God (Long, 'Moral Theology', p. 459). Of course, these are generalizations, and the categories are not mutually exclusive when defined this way, but Long is importantly highlighting the accentuation at work: With such operational definitions, the latter can tend to deontological forms of moral inquiry which in turn draw from modernist assumptions, including the penchant to the generalizable or universal; in contradistinction, the former can draw from a wider range of possibilities which can fund the church's life and witness more readily.

[39] Hauerwas and Wells, 'Why Christian Ethics Was Invented', p. 33.

[40] This notion is repeated by many but sustained definitively in historical framing by D. William Faupel, *The Everlasting Gospel: The Significance of Eschatology in the Development of Pentecostal Thought* (JPTSup 10; Sheffield: Sheffield Academic Press, 1996).

5. A Constructive Operational Rubric: Two Theological Practice-Orientations on the Eschatological Horizon

From this eschatological impulse, one can propose that a way forward for Pentecostalism to reclaim its sense of identity and mission is by way of negotiating more explicitly its doxological practices and the dispositions ensuing from them. Both these practices and dispositions can sustain and perpetuate the Pentecostal ethos in ways that nothing else can because they point to the features of a 'living tradition' that all can see. Such delineations would help Pentecostalism maintain its epicletic form communally by way of making such features as identity and mission ongoing matters of negotiation and embodiment. Of the many options one could choose for dispositions and practices, I find it helpful to propose the category of 'practice-orientations', and to speak of two examples within this category, ones that I label broadly as 'abiding' and 'waiting'.[41]

Why these two? These metaphorical dispositions and outlooks have the distinct advantage of being synergistically indeterminate to some degree. They involve human selves but do so within an acknowledged setting of God's presence and abundant resplendence in all things. As such, 'abiding' and 'waiting' can be said to have active and pathic dimensions,[42] inward- and outward-related convergences. Humans press forward and strive, yet they do so only because of the divine gratuity and the possibilities ensuing from it.

To take the first example, 'abiding' can point to the active side of Pentecostal spirituality, that feature of Pentecostal life in which adherents 'press through' their present struggles and circumstances in order to do all in their power to inhabit the implications ensuing from the divine encounter. The direction of this practice-orientation involves not so much a capitulation to the risk of a

---

[41] I label these 'practice-orientations' because I acknowledge that they lack the kind of specificity appropriate to a theological practice per se. I hope that such broad categorizations can invite a number of imaginative proposals that aim at sustaining a viable communal ethos that is self-generative and resistant to dominant counter-narratives.

[42] I use the term 'pathic' in this study to denote the process of 'undergoing' or 'suffering' an action from another; my use of this term is partly influenced by the general vista found in Reinhard Hütter, *Suffering Divine Things: Theology as Church Practice* (Grand Rapids: Eerdmans, 1999).

'works-righteousness' but rather a heeding of a call to follow and consecrate oneself. The image can also point to the other dimension of synergistic indeterminacy: Abiding retains a pathic dimension because it suggests abiding 'in' or 'alongside' something or someone else. There is a resonance of 'background' to the notion since the term is inherently positional and so relational in some fashion. Both angles, the active and the pathic, are crucial for negotiating a depiction of the Christian life that moves beyond the dyadic, agent-reductive nature of other proposals that depict God and God's creatures as competing or vying for the same power-determinacy. Simply put, abiding is a practice-orientation that acknowledges both the instantiating and continuing need and preeminence of the divine gratuity while recognizing that this gratuity, by the sheer form of its self-communication, requires appropriation and embodied responsiveness.

Within the biblical testimony, the language of 'abiding' or 'remaining' is a Johannine trope particularly emphasized in one of the most pronounced pneumatological sections of Scripture, the 'Farewell Discourse' of John 14-17. The matter pivots significantly on the way the Father is said to be in the Son and the Son in the Father (Jn 14.11), and it is within this dynamic that the Holy Spirit, the one who will abide alongside and be in Christ's disciples, proceeds (Jn 14.17). At play here is a participatory coinherence, one in which Christ's disciples are invited to participate in the triune life of God. But even before the famous vine passage of John 15, one sees a conditionedness already alluded to in John 14 in terms of *keeping Christ's commandments as an expression of love for Christ* (Jn 14.21). The thrust is clear: Abiding is a moral matter in which obedience and responsiveness are imperative.

With the onset of John 15 within the 'Discourse', the reader notices an analogy for the coinherence alluded to in John 14: Jesus is the true vine, the Father is the vinedresser, and the disciples are the branches. Jesus proceeds to command the disciples: 'Abide in me as I abide in you. Just as the branch cannot bear fruit by itself unless it abides in the vine, neither can you unless you abide in me' (Jn 15.4). Through this passage, one sees that the disciples are to find both their identity and sense of flourishing within the dynamic of divine conditionedness: They are nothing apart from the Christ who abides in them through the Spirit. And it is within this dynamic that the disciples are to bear fruit, 'fruit that will last' (Jn 15.16). The 'already' feature of epicletic existence involves an active fruitfulness that is generative to the degree that it is Christ- and Spirit-dependent, that is, coinherently God-oriented. The 'not yet' feature of this way of life is the sense in which the coinherence is continually and variably conditioned to the degree that the disciples keep Christ's commandments. For the disciples, there is always the possibility of failure, one predicated upon human irresponsiveness to the divine call.

The second practice-orientation, 'waiting', is synergistically indeterminate as well since it too can be seen as having both 'active' and 'pathic' dimensions that are often unclear within their phenomenal form as to agential source. The practice of waiting bears resonances with Pentecostal 'tarrying' at the altar. In this practice saints tarry and 'press through' as they seek God through the presentation of their entire selves. And yet, Pentecostals have generally recognized (to what degree is debatable, as the last chapter of this study will press) that for all that they do in preparation for the possibility of divine encounter, such an event is God-initiated and God-sustained. In other words, believers cannot manipulate their way to a transformative moment but have to wait on the manifest presence and work of God. The genuine and enlivening quality of Pentecostal worship is said to occur when 'the Holy Spirit shows up'.

The motif of 'waiting' can be depicted as both Lukan and Pauline. In the case of Luke, the disciples were commanded to wait in Jerusalem for the promise of the Father (Acts 1.4) prior to the events surrounding Pentecost in Acts 2. In their tarrying, the disciples gathered together, prayed, and appointed a successor to Judas before 'the sound like the rush of a violent wind' occurred (Acts 2.2). Their tarrying involved both an open receptivity but also the need to attend to the pressing needs that were at play within the fellowship. In terms of the Pauline depiction of waiting, the motif is prominent in Romans 8, a chapter that begins with Johannine-like themes related to walking according to, being in, and being led by the Spirit. The additional claim related to the Spirit bearing witness with our spirit that we are children of God (Rom. 8.16) also finds a place within these musings. But Paul moves on to relate the difficult side of this Christian life, one that was very much part of his own experience: 'I consider that the sufferings of this present time are not worth comparing with the glory about to be revealed to us. For the creation waits with eager longing for the revealing of the children of God' (Rom. 8.18-19). This tension-laden scenario leads to Paul's notion of the 'groans of creaturely existence', ones that anticipate adoption and redemption in hopefulness. Paul is clear that this process of waiting is not easy: 'For who hopes for what is seen? But if we hope for what we do not see, we wait for it with patience' (Rom. 8.24-25). The difficulty of this waiting is offset by Paul with the comfort and help of the Holy Spirit, the one who intercedes on our behalf 'with sighs too deep for words' (Rom. 8.26). Again, the interplay between divine and human agency is important in the Pauline emphasis on waiting, but now the theological virtue of hope is vital, one that is enabled and sustained by the Spirit as believers peregrinate in what can be a cruel and antagonistic world.

To summarize, the motifs of abiding and waiting are pneumatically conditioned orientations and dispositions, ones that stem from the divine gratuity in such a fashion that the life of the epicletic community is made possible. An interplay between divine agency and human activity and responsiveness makes these practice-orientations generative of grace-filled and character-forming possibilities and instantiations. They beckon an active side of the faith ('abide in me as I abide in you')[43] but in a thoroughly receptive and responsive framing ('apart from me you can do nothing')[44]. Because they are dispositions and orientations that are enabled by and responsive to the divine gratuity, they can lead to a number of what can be termed 'theological practices'.

The notion of theological practices has been deeply inflected by a number of sources, including the work of Alasdair MacIntyre.[45] In his groundbreaking *After Virtue*, MacIntyre defines a practice as

> any coherent and complex form of socially established cooperative human activity through which goods internal to that form of activity are realized in the course of trying to achieve those

---

[43] John 15.4.

[44] John 15.5.

[45] For a collection that employs MacIntyre for theological purposes, see Nancey Murphy, Brad J. Kallenberg, and Mark Thiessen Nation (eds.), *Virtues and Practices in the Christian Tradition: Christian Ethics after MacIntyre* (Harrisburg: Trinity Press International, 1997); see also Miroslav Volf and Dorothy C. Bass (eds.), *Practicing Theology: Beliefs and Practices in Christian Life* (Grand Rapids: Eerdmans, 2002).

standards of excellence which are appropriate to, and partially definitive of, that form of activity, with the result that human powers to achieve excellence, and human conceptions of the ends and goods involved, are systematically extended.[46]

How would the practice-orientations of abiding and waiting be shaped or deepened by MacIntyre's definition?

First, MacIntyre's notion is a collective vision: Practices, in his view, cannot be undertaken alone. The logic extends to abiding and waiting within Christian embodiment: They are practice-orientations that can lead to any number of specific practices that are necessarily undertaken in fellowship. Why is this point important? Part of MacIntyre's logic rests on a retrieval of Aristotelian logic, and in that vision, the good can only be pursued within the context of friendship. As Paul Wadell notes of the Aristotelian framework, 'The one thing that we cannot provide by ourselves is virtue. Aristotle is ruggedly pragmatic about this. Virtue cannot be attained in solitude. By definition it *is* relationship because the virtuous life is the activity of doing good, of practicing good, of developing good habits; and as such, it needs opportunities to be exercised, it demands others on whom the good can be bestowed'.[47] Abiding and waiting, then, if they are to be practice-orientations that guide and shape Pentecostals in their identity as God-fearers and God-lovers, are category headings that can include specific practices that can only be fruitful as 'means of grace'[48] when they are undertaken collectively. If individually pursued, these activities would become something altogether different, leading their practitioners to experience any number of problematic and degenerative corruptions, including possibly a solipsistic spirituality, frustration, despair, and so on.[49]

---

[46] MacIntyre, *After Virtue*, p. 187.

[47] Paul J. Wadell, *Friendship and the Moral Life* (Notre Dame: University of Notre Dame Press, 1989), p. 64. More will be said about virtues in chapter 3.

[48] The allusion here is to the Wesleyan understanding, which will be considered in greater detail in chapter 2.

[49] The point bears repeating: The vision of abiding and waiting offered here requires collective embodiment. To use the MacIntyrean analogy, just like a single person shooting a ball in a hoop is not the game of basketball, so is a person simply 'going at it alone' in the spiritual life, either by sheer force or determination, not the same as abiding or waiting as depicted here. The distinction is crucial because the shift from a worshiping community to a worshiping individual, one that has been increasingly pronounced as Pentecostalism has become more

Tied to this emphasis on a collective undertaking is a second notion that practices, if they strive toward a form of excellence appropriate to their ends, require performance and embodiment for them to be understood in their many dimensions. Consequently, the practice-orientations of abiding and waiting are to be envisioned as collectively fostered dispositions that require a praxis-register for including and sustaining them; in other words, they can only be appreciated when they are on display through the specificity of particular activities. Simply put, there is no substitute for witnessing and living into the theological practices of a Christian form of life. And as people cultivate these dispositions, they will come to see what their goal is and how to live into it increasingly and more excellently. For Pentecostals, as for all Christians generally, the standard of excellence involves the call to be holy as the God of Israel is holy (Lev. 19.2), to be perfect (*teleios*) as Jesus and our Father is perfect (Mt. 5.48). The theological practice-orientations of abiding and waiting point to sanctification, that mode of being that corresponds to the form of Christ and so that will mark beatitude.

Third, with MacIntyre's definition highlighting the notion of excellence, one can see that practices point to the goods associated with a given collective and in turn seek to promote the activities and habits necessary for these goods to be extended across time and space. Pentecostals have the stereotype of being exceedingly inept in catechesis, but part of that difficulty rests on Pentecostals implicitly recognizing the limits of catechesis if what is meant by such a task is propositional memorization and recall. Pentecostalism has sustained the catechetical task but in a manner that is invitational and aesthetic. In Pentecostal catechesis, onlookers are bidden to 'come and see' the sights, sounds, and wonders of Pentecostal worship. What the emphases of abiding and waiting point to is the good highlighted by the Pentecostal ethos, namely the encounter between God and humanity, one that can be either delightful or crushing but always with the aim of being reparative, transformative, and empowering. From this encounter, one that believers con-

---

mainstream and so Evangelical, has worked against the perpetuation of the Pentecostal way of life. Pentecostalism has never been about privatized religious experience or gnostic propositional content. As in the Book of Acts, so at Azusa and beyond: Pentecost is an outward-directed gesture, one best characterized as an outpouring of God's Spirit upon God's creation for purposes of restoring and healing it in this 'time-between-the-times'.

tinually abide in and wait for within the doxological modality of Pentecostal worship, the goal of the Christian life becomes ever-clearer: greater conformity and likeness to the triune God. The practice-orientations of abiding and waiting then point to the escha-tologically conditioned shape of the Christian life.

6. Looking Ahead

The Pentecostal Movement as a whole would benefit from the em-phases of abiding and waiting since these practice-orientations stem from features inherent to Pentecostal worship. Nevertheless, if a Pentecostal ethic is pursued and such framing is most appropriately situated within the rubric of moral theology (given the centrality of Pentecostal worship for Pentecostal identity), then a pressing matter for the Pentecostal Movement is the need to locate itself as a sub-tradition within the church catholic, a move that is difficult to ac-commodate given its revivalist orientation.[50] The move may sound counter-intuitive, but the options are deleterious: Movements come and go, yet Pentecostalism continues to carry on, moving into a formal second century of existence. Reification of past forms is not an option with changing times but neither is a thoughtless or rushed accommodation if central features of that identity are to perdure. All these concerns reach an even more heightened sense with the recognition that American Pentecostalism has already ex-perienced a wide range of institutionalization: Pentecostals are al-ready 'churchly' in terms of having statements of faith, educational institutions, ordination processes, and so forth, yet the denial of

---

[50] To press the matter a bit further, one could say that one of the persistent difficulties of a revivalist context is that the end is usually an individual's trans-formation, a privileging which buys into the changes wrought by the modernist revolution of Descartes, Kant, and others. However, the individualism of revival-ist fervor, one which Pentecostals have imbibed considerably, has started to run its course, making a renegotiation of the location and end of transformation a considerable matter. I sympathize with Hütter's call to shift the paradigm, from thinking of the subject as the end of the church to holding to the church as the end of the subject (see his chapter 'The Church', in Buckley and Yeago [eds.], *Knowing the Triune God*, p. 25). The application of this sensibility within the Pente-costal fold could be extended through the following phrasing: Believers do not have the Holy Spirit, but the Holy Spirit has them; therefore, in extending this logic to the epicletic community, one could say that believers do not simply con-stitute the church but that the church in important ways constitutes believers.

these as distinctly ecclesial elements (which would mean, among many things, a more self-aware and actively pursued sense of ecumenicity) for the sake of maintaining a movement-mentality can only impede the maturation of the subtradition as a whole.

In light of these concerns, the present work will promote the practice-orientations of abiding and waiting within the contexts of two frameworks associated with Christian moral reflection that have been heralded repeatedly for their salutary implications for the church; these are the affections and virtues. In both cases, an interplay between divine and human agency is key, and the documentation and elaboration of their pneumatological interplay can only help in negotiating the doxological-eschatological modality enacted in Pentecostal witness and life. These sensibilities developed in Chapters 2 and 3 will further be on display regarding two crucial points related to Pentecostal theological ethics: how 'bearing fruit' could look like within the Pentecostal fold in light of the capitulation and pressure toward holiness codification (Chapter 4) and the transformation of Pentecostal eschatological urgency in light of Christ's tarrying (Chapter 5).

2

ABIDING AND WAITING AS DISPOSITIONS OF THE HEART

Jonathan Edwards famously remarked that 'True religion, in great part, consists in holy affections'.[1] Given Wesley's abridgment and endorsement of Edwards' treatise, one could say that the Englishman was of the same opinion.[2] The language of interiority was important for these revivalists in that they sensed that through the encounter with God something had to change at the very core of one's being. Interiority and its many terminological negotiations within Christian circles were of importance to these preachers who knew that expressions of beauty as well as chicanery were possible during altar moments. Rather than belaboring the details of the inner dynamics of religious experience, Edwards believed that 'conversion is best studied in terms of its effects rather than its means', thereby leading him to consider the affections as providing 'the most ascertainable index of these effects'.[3] Edwards knew that a real conversion would produce effects that were evident to those willing to notice, and he legitimately believed there was a particular uniformity to these outcomes, one based on their common source:

---

[1] Jonathan Edwards, *The Works of Jonathan Edwards, volume 2: Religious Affections* (ed., John E. Smith; New Haven: Yale University Press, 1959), p. 95.

[2] See Gregory S. Clapper, '"True Religion" and the Affections: A Study of John Wesley's Abridgement of Jonathan Edwards' *Treatise on Religious Affections*', *Wesleyan Theological Journal* 19 (1984), pp. 77-89. See also the larger work by Richard B. Steele, *'Gracious Affection' and 'True Virtue' according to Jonathan Edwards and John Wesley* (Metuchen: Scarecrow, 1994).

[3] William J. Scheick, *The Writings of Jonathan Edwards* (College Station: Texas A & M University Press, 1975), p. 88.

the work of the Holy Spirit. Edwards' context is important for understanding the emphasis he gives to discernment, for 'America's theologian' witnessed both the spiritual vibrancy and the emotional and psychomotor aberrations and duplicity associated with the Great Awakening. Consequently, Edwards wished to grant a place for religious experience but only within the parameters of certain criteria that could aid in the discernment of the Holy Spirit's activity.

Pentecostalism's priorities would run similarly. If Pentecostalism is a doxological way of life, then it would be important to incorporate methods and frameworks that attempt to discern true from false religious experience when the subtradition is assessed and evaluated. Pentecostals have always believed it important to discern the legitimacy of claims and experiences by the way one leads one's life. These practical considerations make the broader rubric of spirituality very appealing for considering and categorizing the Pentecostal ethos, for this notion attends not only to proper beliefs but also to worthwhile and coherent actions. Both of these emphases inevitably suggest, either implicitly or explicitly, the interiority, character, and condition of the agents in question. After all, beliefs are adhered to because in some manner they are found to be compelling to the point that people 'make the leap' to hold them; furthermore, one's actions stem from one being compelled by a good that leads one to seek and act in conformity with it. Broadly, Christian spirituality has in its purview the integration of beliefs, practices, and the dimension of interiority characteristic of being human. Out of convenience, many have offered trichotomous sets of tropes to indicate this dynamic, including 'mind – soul – body' or 'head – heart – hands'. One that more recently has garnered significant attention among Pentecostals in light of Steven Land's proposals has been the Wesleyan understanding of 'knowing – being – doing', or more specifically 'right beliefs – right affections – right actions'. The last set can also be spoken of as 'orthodoxy – orthopathy – orthopraxy'.[4] One may think that the normative dimensions of these tropes would be easy enough to consider, but on closer inspection, they are notoriously difficult to delineate.

---

[4] For a helpful introduction to these terms, see Richard B. Steele's 'Introduction' to his edited volume, *'Heart Religion' in the Methodist Tradition and Related Movements* (Lanham: Scarecrow, 2001), pp. xix-xlv.

For instance, since the words in the last set share the same prefix ('ortho-'), it is worth asking what precisely determines their normative quality and how they may be so. What is the normative framework at play for negotiating what is true from false beliefs or practices? Heresy is not a topic that is easily broached in a culture that values political correctness, and yet Christians, if they claim a category such as 'orthodoxy', imply that heresy does exist and so should be identified and avoided. Furthermore, what would constitute 'right' Christian action in the world? What concrete activities stem from the Christian conviction of being 'salt' of the earth and 'light' in the world?

If these questions are difficult to sustain with regard to beliefs and practices, they are even more complex to consider in terms of the interiority of agents, and this difficulty is largely attributable to the ambiguity and conflationary impulses surrounding the 'language of the heart'. For instance, in English itself, the term 'emotion' is a relatively new invention, one that was privileged in the nineteenth century and that in turn has functioned as a 'catch-all' category for words such as 'tempers', 'affections', 'feelings', and others that were in circulation in previous centuries.[5] The rise of the term 'emotion' points to transitions that took place in English in relation to the categorization of human affectivity, making such language problematic at best and possibly unsustainable at worst because of incompatible assumptions about what is at work in such speech. If the referents are not agreed upon, then neither can the discourse proceed coherently. Given the transitions that took place within the philosophical and cultural conventions of the Anglophone world in relation to human interiority, the linguistic and referential constructs were bound to change as well.

Pentecostals have had something at stake in establishing a workable account of human interiority, for the logic of Pentecostalism's way of life depends upon it. Rather than relying on intuitions or anecdotal evidence, Pentecostals have found it important to register the interior dynamics and outcomes of the transformative encoun-

---

[5] See Thomas Dixon, *From Passions to Emotions: The Creation of a Secular Psychological Category* (Cambridge: Cambridge University Press, 2003). A fascinating hypothesis that Dixon entertains as one of the reasons for this shift is the secularization of modern psychology within this time period. The category of 'emotions' had a generalizable appeal at this time that other past terms did not because of the latter's association with religious (particularly Christian) beliefs (see pp. 4-5).

ter with God in some generalizable way, and usually, this approach has been in terms of human affectivity. At least two important accounts of affectivity have emerged by Pentecostals: the proposals by Samuel Solivan and Steven Land. In what follows, these accounts will be surveyed and then situated within the larger parameters and discussions surrounding the reception of eighteenth century revivalism (particularly as embodied in the work of John Wesley) for the purposes of suggesting in a sustained way the kinds of transformative affective features that can be understood to be part of a Pentecostal moral theology that approaches being-in-the-world epicletically as a dynamic of abiding and waiting.

1. Samuel Solivan and Orthopathos

During the early part of the 1990s, two Pentecostal scholars offered proposals for substantiating what is 'right' about the kind of affectivity resulting from the Pentecostal way of life. Solivan himself acknowledged the serendipity; in surveying briefly Land's proposals, Solivan narrates:

> Land goes on to state that these 'affections are abiding dispositions which dispose the person toward God and the neighbor in ways appropriate to their source and goal in God'. It is the issue of disposition toward neighbor that I wish to attend to in my use of the term *orthopathos*. I should note that both Steven Land and I developed our use of the terms 'orthopathy' and 'orthopathos' independently of each other. I am convinced that orthopathy and *orthopathos*, taken together, comprise a more integrative understanding of Pentecostal spirituality in its pneumatic and social context.[6]

From this remark, one can see that Solivan finds his and Land's proposals to be complementary. In Solivan's way of thinking, his work seeks to extend a certain logic of Pentecostal affectivity in terms of the neighbor (that is, the social context) in a way that

---

[6] Samuel Solivan, *The Spirit, Pathos and Liberation: Toward an Hispanic Pentecostal Theology* (JPTSup 14; Sheffield: Sheffield Academic Press, 1998), pp. 12-13, citing Land, *Pentecostal Spirituality*, p. 136; an earlier article by Solivan introduces the notion of orthopathos; see Samuel Solivan, 'Orthopathos: Interlocutor between Orthodoxy and Praxis', *Andover Newton Review* 1 (1990), pp. 19-25.

Land's may not in an overt manner. This judgment of complementarity is worth exploring in order that it may become clearer what Pentecostals believe is normative in terms of a workable account of human affectivity stemming from the Pentecostal ethos.

Solivan writes as a 'New Yorican' (a person living or raised in New York who has links to Puerto Rico) who has ministered in challenging urban contexts. In a way reminiscent of liberation theology more generally, Solivan theologizes from the experiences he has had in the 'barrio'. His concerns, interests, and allegiances do not lie with theologically speculative and abstract notions (that is, those ways of theologizing that stem from European and Eurocentric modes) but with the everyday lives of those who suffer on the margins of society, particularly those who endure the Hispanic-American reality within the North American context. In turn, undeniably humane and authentic features of Solivan's project are immediately on display in his work: The plight of his community is very much on his mind as he theologizes.

The notion of orthopathos emerges for Solivan because of the limits he sees with the other two 'orthos' as they have been negotiated in formal academic theology. On the one hand, in the case of orthodoxy, he finds that attempts to strive for propositionally 'right doctrine' have done little by way of alleviating the suffering of the poor and disenfranchised. Orthopraxis, on the other hand, has become an academically fashionable theme that is often pursued by onlookers of those who are actually engaged in hands-on activity. These onlookers lack, in Solivan's mind, an 'existential link to the poor'.[7] Therefore, Solivan is hoping to sidestep the shortcomings of both 'orthos' as they have popularly been negotiated through his account of orthopathos, one that assumes a kind of pathos that involves 'a people's suffering, dehumanization, pain and marginalization'.[8] With this pathos in mind, Solivan can say that what 'rectifies' or heals it is the presence and work of the Holy Spirit: Orthopathos is 'the power of the Holy Spirit in one's life that transforms pathos, suffering and despair into hope and wholeness. Orthopathos is that holistic, liberating process that engenders hope in … suffering'.[9] It

---

[7] Solivan, *The Spirit, Pathos and Liberation*, p. 36.
[8] Solivan, *The Spirit, Pathos and Liberation*, p. 12.
[9] Solivan, *The Spirit, Pathos and Liberation*, pp. 27-28.

brings 'empathic concern for the sufferer into the act of doing the-ology'.[10]

Orthopathos, therefore, is on display in the work of the triune God within the economy of salvation. According to Solivan, the incarnation is a 'watershed in the transformative possibilities of pa-thos'.[11] This work of God in turn raises an 'orthopathic conscious-ness' among the suffering and those beholding them in that the op-pressed, marginalized, and dehumanized can come to understand and deal with their pathos in a way that they can 'overcome their situation [and] not wallow in it'.[12] What transforms pathos, then, is a liberative and redemptive content or insight, one that is spurred by a pneumatological transformation that is referenced according to Solivan in biblical passages such as Jn 1.14 and Rom. 8.2.

What to make of Solivan's proposals? First of all, it is clear that pathos in his mind relates to a social reality, one of marginalization and dehumanization. In this sense, the context in question is very particular: Pathos is tied to the experience of fallen structures and their deleterious consequences upon human life. Therefore, this pathos requires redemption and healing, and this process of moving from self-alienating to redemptive suffering marks the pneumato-logical transformation assumed in orthopathos. This pathos appar-ently is available to both the sufferer and the onlooker of suffering, and in both cases the transition to hope is salutary so that the con-ditions and circumstances surrounding such pathos will not be wholly destructive.

Second, Solivan's assumed accounts of both sin and salvation are tied to liberationist concerns. Sin is largely a structural matter, and salvation is considerably portrayed as a liberative process in which those structural conditions are recognized for what they are so that such recognitions can provide the occasions and empower-ment necessary for enduring and working against them.[13] On the

---

[10] Solivan, *The Spirit, Pathos and Liberation*, p. 60.

[11] Solivan, *The Spirit, Pathos and Liberation*, p. 61.

[12] Solivan, *The Spirit, Pathos and Liberation*, p. 62.

[13] Solivan's is not a wholesale liberationist account, for he explicitly remarks that '*Orthopathos* as used [in his work] is not a direct equivalent of liberation' (Solivan, *The Spirit, Pathos and Liberation*, p. 65); therefore, orthopathos does not so much imply a program for social change but a spiritual dimension that 'em-powers sufferers for the long-term with their present, and often long-term, con-ditions' (p. 65).

one hand, this account is helpful in raising consciousness of the degree and extent of pathos throughout the fallen world. The point is especially needed in academic culture where privilege and abstraction have a way of overshadowing the plight of the majority world. At the same time, liberationist portrayals of sin and salvation run a risk of reduction, for sin is more than fallen social structures and salvation is more than coming to an insight of one's dignity and value in light of God's presence and work. No doubt the features of sin and salvation that Solivan assumes are integral to any extensive account of each, but on their own, they are insufficient to account for their complex biblical portrayal.

Third, and most pressingly, the transition from pathos to orthopathos is not entirely clear in Solivan's proposals. He does acknowledge that the transition involves greater insight, consciousness, and empowerment and that these are products of the Spirit's work (which includes the specific act of identification) and of human repentance, but outside of these general claims, the movement appears largely underdeveloped. Several questions could be pressed in light of this ambiguity, including: Where and how does this transition take place? Within what modality and under what conditions would the movement best be facilitated? How does one account for the apathy that marks those who are not immediately touched by the pathos in question? What does the existence of such apathy say about the human condition and its possibilities? In what way is orthopathos tied to the ends of a Christian and to beatitude more generally? All these questions in one way or another point to the most glaring oversight in Solivan's work, namely a workable and to some degree extensive account of human affectivity. Solivan does try to offer this in his explicit gestures of how orthopathos is primordially a disposition of God that is extendable to humanity in that the latter is created in the *imago Dei*, yet if pathos is strictly defined in terms of brokenness, one wonders about those aspects of the affectional life, both divine and human, that do not directly correspond to this feature of human brokenness. In other words, Solivan's account of pathos is but one feature or constituent element of human affectivity, but to reduce the latter to the former would be a bit rushed. One senses in Solivan's offerings that the fall overdetermines the creational impetus of God's original purposes for humanity, and as such, the transition from pathos to orthopathos is significantly complicated as a result. The normativity implied by the 'ortho' in Solivan's account of orthopathos is framed as reactionary and dependent on post-fall conditions.

In summary, Solivan is right to point out that Pentecostalism carries with it an appeal to the masses, especially to those who have been marginalized and set aside by the powers that be. One cannot deny that the Pentecostal message and way of life have the potential to dignify and empower their participants in holistic ways, making them realize their value in Christ and their potential role within the economy of God's salvation. Nevertheless, the experience of oppression and its reconfiguration in acts of liberation and humanization are themselves insufficient to generate a normative account of human affectivity, one that could function within an expression of Pentecostal moral theology. Despite the constructive appeal of Solivan's work, more appears to be required to account for the logic of affective transformation within the Pentecostal ethos.

2. Steven Land and Orthopathy

Steven Land's *Pentecostal Spirituality* has been an important work in Pentecostal studies, not simply because it was the first volume of the *Journal of Pentecostal Theology Supplement Series* but more so in terms of its recasting of the Pentecostal Movement as a spirituality. Of course, spirituality as a theologically serious and generative category has gained in prominence within academic circles since the publication of *Pentecostal Spirituality*, but the acceptance of 'spirituality' for sustained theological consideration was contested at the time of Land's book.

Of the many features of Land's project that have proven generative, one has been its emphasis on orthopathy. Land's understanding of a normative account of human affectivity draws broadly from the resources of evangelical piety, particularly John Wesley and Jonathan Edwards, but its specific dependence is upon the work of Theodore Runyon, a scholar in the Methodist tradition who uses the term to describe part of the dynamic inherent to the Methodist revival of the eighteenth century. Runyon's account of orthopathic religious experience involves several features, including its source and end/telos as well as its accompanying transformation and feelings.[14] Drawing on such figures as Runyon, Don Saliers, Gregory Clapper, and Henry Knight III, Land makes a vital link:

> [*Pentecostal Spirituality*] uses 'orthopathy' to refer to the affections which motivate the heart and characterize the believer. As shown by Saliers, Clapper and Knight, the Christian affections are the heart of the spirituality of Edwards and Wesley. They are likewise the heart of Pentecostal spirituality.[15]

For Land, the integrating center between orthodoxy and orthopraxy is orthopathy, and the latter is constituted by 'distinctive affections which are belief shaped, praxis oriented and characteristic of a person'.[16] Like Solivan, Land sees Pentecostalism, along with other Christian traditions (particularly African-American and Wesleyan-Holiness trajectories), favoring a kind of affective epistemology or rationality rather than a propositionalist kind. This affective integrating center is part and parcel of the early Pentecostal emphasis on an 'experiential primitivism', one that was eschatologically framed and that in turn coalesced with an 'ecclesiastical primitivism' (a suspicion of institutional accoutrements, like creeds) and an 'ethical primitivism', one that 'called [early Pentecostals] to an all-consuming passion for holiness'.[17]

With various references to the Azusa periodical *The Apostolic Faith*, Land recalls how for early Pentecostals, living into the Pentecostal way of life was very much a praxis-oriented concern, one that involved the cultivation and fostering of certain dispositions and attitudes, and these, he remarks, fell under the category of the 'fruit of the Spirit'; as Land states, 'The character or fruit of the Spirit that should, according to Seymour, characterize those early persecuted witnesses are analyzed in this [third chapter of *Pentecostal Spirituality*] as Pentecostal affections'.[18] He continues in suggesting that the participation in Pentecostal narratives and practices (what com-

---

[14] Runyon's early works on 'orthopathy' that would have been available to Land include Theodore Runyon, 'A New Look at "Experience"', *Drew Gateway* 57 (1988), pp. 44-55, and *idem*, 'The Importance of Experience for Faith', in Randy L. Maddox (ed.), *Aldersgate Reconsidered* (Nashville: Kingswood, 1990), pp. 93-107. More recent works from Runyon will be explored below.

[15] Land, *Pentecostal Spirituality*, p. 44.

[16] Land, *Pentecostal Spirituality*, p. 44.

[17] Land, *Pentecostal Spirituality*, p. 60.

[18] Land, *Pentecostal Spirituality*, pp. 124-25.

bined would be denominated in the present study as its 'way of life') enables an 'affective transformation', one that can be elaborated in terms of a correlation of certain divine attributes, an apocalyptic vision of Christ's reign, and the experiential testimony of an individual.[19]

From this correlation, Land's account of the affections rests on the Pentecostal believer's growing participation in conformity to the triune God. Through the 'three crises model', Land shows how this maturation process could be theologically described, and in turn, he provides an explicitly theological grounding and end (the triune God) to his account of orthopathy as a well as a context and modality in which it is cultivated (prayerful and worshipful receptivity and praxis by the attendant missionary fellowship of believers). In summarizing this dynamic, Land mentions that 'Christian affections are objective, relational, and dispositional'.[20] They are objective in that they have a proper object (source and end), the triune God. They are relational in that they 'require for their proper genesis and ongoing expression a relationship with God, the church and the world'.[21] And they are dispositional in that they relate to 'abiding' attitudes that characterize and shape a person so that they construe and interact with the world in a distinct way.[22] Aware of the pitfalls of attempting an 'exhaustive analysis' and a 'reductionistic essentialization', Land moves to offer three examples of Pentecostal affections (gratitude, compassion, and courage) and proceeds to offer a correlational schematization in which these affections are placed within a larger rubric that entails both God's character and the dynamics of salvation within God's economy.

Land's account of orthopathy is significantly nuanced and theologically rich. His normative portrayal of Christian affectivity can draw from the gifts of the Wesleyan-Methodist tradition, and in doing so, it can account for a number of features that Solivan's constructive account cannot. Land's link between the affections and the fruit of the Spirit furthermore adds scriptural warrants to his project that are more compelling than Solivan's more broadly thematic overtures. Nevertheless, whereas Solivan's focus on the poor

---

[19] Land, *Pentecostal Spirituality*, p. 125.
[20] Land, *Pentecostal Spirituality*, p. 134.
[21] Land, *Pentecostal Spirituality*, p. 135.
[22] Land, *Pentecostal Spirituality*, p. 136.

and marginalized may be a reduction of sorts, it does provide a certain level of concretization that would have helped strengthen Land's approach. Despite the specificity on offer in the highlighting of the three affections he chooses, Land's elaboration of these still appears at times a bit too abstract and perhaps idealized. Furthermore, at several points Land's portrayal of the affections sounds quite similar to a portrayal of the Christian virtues, a move that is quite easy to make, and yet a case can be made that these two moral frameworks are distinguishable both in form and logic. Finally, and this point has been sustained by many, Land's offering generally does little by way of accentuating baptism in the Holy Spirit, the one topic that American Pentecostals have tended to emphasize considerably throughout their history for purposes of identity negotiation.

3. *Ad fontes*: The Wesleyan Contribution

Both Solivan and Land employ an understanding of a normative account of human affectivity as the bridge or interactive element between normative dimensions of faith and practice. In other words, they assume the 'three orthos' in order to render their account of the Pentecostal ethos. Such a schematization bears strong resemblance to the Wesleyan vision of the Christian life. For instance, one notes that Land appeals to a number of Methodist scholars for elaborating his own proposals. Also, Solivan prefers a broadly and loosely liberationist framework, but he readily recognizes the difficulty of using pathos language within that particular theological model.[23] Given Land's uses and Solivan's reservations, one could be spurred to delve deeper into the Wesleyan tradition on human affectivity since normative affectivity (one could say 'heart religion') within this church family has a rich and extensive line of reflection. The purpose of such an exploration would be to nuance further and develop what would be involved in an account of normative religious affectivity within the Pentecostal fold so as to make such a framework generative for proposals related to constructive measures for Pentecostal moral theology.

---

[23] Solivan remarks, 'For many the introduction and utilization of the term "pathos" seem inappropriate and out of place in a discussion of liberation' (Solivan, 'Orthopathos', p. 20).

Two Wesleyan scholars in particular have offered elaborations of what normative affectivity would look like given the sensibilities at play within the Wesleyan *via salutis*: Theodore Runyon and his proposals related to 'orthopathy' and Gregory Clapper's notion of *orthokardia*. Although differences exist between these two scholars, their interpretations of Wesley's privileging of 'heart religion' significantly overlap. When one inductively follows the logic of Wesley's understanding of the affections, what becomes evidently clear is that they are the locus of embodied holiness for Wesley; they represent the marks of 'real change' in a believer's life. In fact, according to Clapper, Wesley understood a life marked by the religious affections as 'essential to Christianity'.[24]

What then is involved in a rendering of Wesley's understanding of the normative character of the religious affections? In Wesleyan key, what gives these affections their 'ortho' character? Runyon has repeatedly mentioned several qualities.[25] First of all, one can see that there is a clear sense that the religious affections have their source in the triune God. This move is important for several reasons, not the least of which relates to its assumptions and implications for religious epistemology. Because of Wesley's understanding that the object of Christian experience is outside of the self, some have remarked that his religious epistemology owes its logic to the Lockean empiricism of the time. Whatever its source,[26] clearly Wesley is quite different from Schleiermacher and others who would

---

[24] Gregory S. Clapper, *The Renewal of the Heart is the Mission of the Church* (Eugene: Cascade, 2011), p. 4. In an elaboration of Wesley's 'Plain Account of Genuine Christianity' (where Wesley speaks of humility, gratitude, love, and other affections), Clapper remarks: '[Wesley] begins this account of "genuine Christianity", then, by first writing about what the personal enfleshment of Christianity looks like, and he expresses this in terms of the affections or tempers of the heart. Only *after* this is done does he turn to discussing what Christianity itself is' (p. 13).

[25] What follows draws from Theodore Runyon, *The New Creation: John Wesley's Theology Today* (Nashville: Abingdon, 1998), chapter 5; much of this material was reprinted in the chapter Theodore Runyon, 'Orthopathy: Wesleyan Criteria for Religious Experience', in Steele (ed.), *'Heart Religion' in the Methodist Tradition and Related Movements*, pp. 291-305.

[26] Often in these discussions the figure of Peter Browne also makes its way as a potential source for Wesley's religious epistemology, but others present themselves, including John Norris and Nicholas Malebranche; see Rex D. Matthews, '"With the Eyes of Faith": Spiritual Experience and the Knowledge of God in the Theology of John Wesley', in Theodore Runyon (ed.), *Wesleyan Theology Today: A Bicentennial Theological Consultation* (Nashville: Kingswood, 1985), pp. 406-15.

suggest otherwise, namely that religious experience is more of a subjective phenomenon, one that is prompted and intuited within the natural conditions of the self. Wesley's views were more aligned to the notion that the mind has a more 'passive role of receiving ordering, and reflecting upon the information provided it by the senses'.[27] In Wesley's opinion, religious experience – as the experience *of God* – must 'transcend subjectivism'; as Runyon notes,

> For Wesley's Lockean approach ... experience functions to register the reality of a spiritual world that transcends the self. The focus in religious experience is upon the Other, and upon the self only as it serves as the object of the Other and the necessary receptor of experience. The impressions made upon its spiritual senses enable the self to reflect upon the reality of the Other.[28]

When Wesley talks about the 'spiritual senses', he means ones that are awakened and vivified by the work of God in one's life; it is through the prompting of these that believers have 'eyes to see' and 'ears to hear' the mighty works of God. Wesley thoroughly believed that the Spirit's work was perceptible, as is evident in one of his most oft-quoted passages of Scripture, Rom. 8.16.[29] Because the language of 'seeing' and 'hearing' is repeatedly used in the Bible for the apprehension of spiritual realities, these epistemological patterns can be said to have biblical corollaries as well as touch-points to sundry materials from Christian antiquity. These 'spiritual senses' are created capacities that God gives humans but that in turn have been 'dulled by the Fall and the habits of sin and indifference'.[30] As a consequence of this logic, one can say that regenerated believers simply 'see' things they did not in their sinful states. The fallen con-

---

[27] Runyon, 'The Importance of Experience for Faith', p. 95.

[28] Theodore Runyon, *The New Creation*, p. 161. These claims are simply counterintuitive to contemporary sensibilities, but they are important. Another way Runyon makes the case is the following: 'Strictly speaking, genuine experience of God is not *my* experience, it is the experience of the Other into whose life I am taken by grace. It is a *shared* reality. Presumptuous as it may seem, we are allowed to share in *God's* experience' (p. 162; emphases in original).

[29] In light of this reasoning, Wesley's understanding of Christian assurance has links with his epistemology of religious experience as it relates to the spiritual senses; see Runyon, 'Orthopathy', p. 292.

[30] Runyon, 'The Importance of Experience for Faith', p. 96.

dition of sinners, in other words, contributes to a disablement of their spiritual sense perception.[31] As Wesley illustrates the point,

> While a man is in a mere natural state, before he is born of God, he has, in a spiritual sense, eyes and sees not … His other spiritual senses are all locked up … Therefore, though he is a living man, he is a dead Christian. But as soon as he is born of God there is a total change in all these particulars. The 'eyes of his understanding are opened'.[32]

The religious affections also have a particular *telos* in Wesley's perspective, and this end is to have the 'mind of Christ'.[33] For all the difficulty associated with Wesley's understanding of Christian perfection, it at least means this much: to be conformed to God's holy self as on display in the life of Christ. Such an understanding creates a number of possible similarities between deification in Eastern Orthodoxy and Wesley's view of Christian perfection, but more to the point for purposes related to this study: One can only aspire to 'right beliefs' and 'right practices' when these are prompted and cultivated by 'right affections', and the concretization and exemplification of this normativity is found in the person of Christ.

To have the 'mind of Christ' then is to undergo a definitive transformation. The awakening of the 'spiritual senses' and the cultivation of the religious affections mean that a person undergoes not only a 'relative change' (one of status or identity) in relation to God, but a 'real change' at the core of one's being.[34] In a sense, one does not have such an experience but the experience produces the self.[35] As Maddox remarks, 'The defining goal of Wesley's heart re-

---

[31] See Richard P. Heitzenrater, 'God with Us: Grace and the Spiritual Senses in John Wesley's Theology', in Robert K. Johnston, L. Gregory Jones, and Jonathan R. Wilson (eds.), *Grace upon Grace: Essays in Honor of Thomas A. Langford* (Nashville: Abingdon, 1999), pp. 87-109.

[32] 'The New Birth', II, p. 192; sermons from the Wesleyan corpus will be from the Bicentennial Edition (*The Works of John Wesley, volumes 1-4* [ed. Albert C. Outler; Nashville: Abingdon, 1984-1987]), and each reference will be marked by sermon title, volume number, and page number.

[33] This is but one expression Wesley uses to describe the condition or dynamic of Christian perfection; it is found prominently in 'The New Birth', among other places.

[34] Examples of this turn of phrase can be found in 'Justification by Faith', I, p. 187; 'The Great Privilege of Those that are Born of God', I, pp. 431-32; 'The Scripture Way of Salvation', II, p. 158; and 'The New Birth', II, p. 187.

[35] Runyon, *The New Creation*, p. 163.

ligion was clearly [a] *change of affections*.[36] This work of transformation is primarily understood as a pneumatological achievement. The believer is awakened and vivified by the presence and work of the Holy Spirit. In fact, part of the testing of religious experience involves the measure to which one is changed, for if the work was of the Spirit, change – at least at the instantiating moment – would necessarily take place.[37]

Furthermore, if such experiences of transformation can be tested and adjudicated, then in some sense they have to be rational. Wesley repeatedly stated throughout his life that faith is always consistent with reason.[38] Undoubtedly, this proclivity of Wesley stems in part from his Enlightenment context of the eighteenth century. At the same time, the Bible repeatedly warns God's people to test and discern (for example, 1 Jn 4.1), and these activities are rational in some sense. Therefore, Wesley was of the opinion that 'orthopathic experience' has to fit within a broader interpretive rubric. The validity of Christian religious experience rests not only in that it is experience of one who transcends the subject but it also is undergone or 'suffered' within a community of interpretation that can discern and interpret it.[39] Otherwise, one is left with little by way of

---

[36] R. Maddox, 'A Change in Affections: The Development, Dynamics, and Dethronement of John Wesley's Heart Religion', in Steele (ed.), *'Heart Religion' in the Methodist Tradition and Related Movements*, p. 17 (emphasis in original).

[37] Fitting here is Runyon's citation of Martin Buber's quote that one 'does not pass from the moment of supreme meeting the same being as he entered into it' (*I and Thou* [Edinburgh: T & T Clark, 1937], p. 109 as quoted in Runyon, *The New Creation*, p. 163). No doubt such sensibilities stem in part from the Old Testament depictions of divine-human encounter, especially the examples of the prophets. Naturally, people can choose either to live into or deny the results of these transformative encounters, a reality that points once again to the synergistic shape of this vision.

[38] 'The Case of Reason Impartially Considered', II, p. 593.

[39] Runyon, *The New Creation*, p. 161. Clapper believes that of George Lindbeck's tripartite typology in *The Nature of Doctrine: Religion and Theology in a Postliberal Age* (Philadelphia: Westminster, 1984), the one most fitting for Wesley is the cultural-linguistic model (rather than the experiential-expressivist one) in that the normative or patterned nature of Christian affectivity and its interpretation as such take place in community (see Gregory S. Clapper, *John Wesley on Religious Affections: His Views on Experience and Emotion and Their Role in the Christian Life and Theology* [Metuchen: Scarecrow, 1989], pp. 156-58, 160). Although it is not clear to what degree one can make the connection between Wesleyanism and the cultural-linguistic model, more important here is to demarcate without equivocation that the experiential-expressivist type does not apply to Wesley and his heirs despite the fact that both emphasize 'experience'. Simply put, the understandings

making sense of the interior life. Precisely in this aspect of ascertaining coherence and consistency is the value of orthodoxy: The testimony and teaching of the church serve as reliable, time-tested, and meaning-generative hermeneutical frameworks by which to situate religious experiences.

Orthopathic experience is also directed outward and so could be labeled as social. Once again, the goal of religious experience is not to have an experience for one to enjoy solipsistically in a commodified and consumerist fashion. The transformation implied by the Spirit's work of recreation and healing is for the purpose of renewing the cosmos. As beneficiaries of such work, Christians are called to extend it, and such an understanding creates the vital link between orthopathy and orthopraxy. In an important sense, 'right works require a right heart' and 'a right heart should prompt right works'.[40] Without this practical dimension, the orthopathic experience devolves into something other than what it was meant to be. For this reason, orthopathy and the religious affections are relevant for the task of moral theology, for they suggest in Wesleyan key what is distinctive about Spirit-enabled being-in-the-world as it stems from the divine encounter.

Finally, Runyon speaks of the affections as being 'sacramental'.[41] By the latter, Runyon is appealing to the interactivity between mind and body. Wesley did not hold to a latent gnosticism or a Platonic privileging of the soul. Materiality and embodiment are important in that they are features of the incarnation. The appeal to Christ as a normative center is possible because Christ was a particular human being who led a life on display before others. If Christ is the true sacrament, then his body displays a kind of sacramental existence, not simply by its existence per se but more definitively and deeply by its evident shape and character.

This emphasis on sacramentality points to another dimension of the Wesleyan vision of orthopathy, and that is the means of grace. Wesley used the trope 'means of grace' to designate those practices that are assumed to be part of a vibrant life that is actively and pas-

---

of religious experience between what Lindbeck envisions with his second category and the Wesleyan logic are emphatically disparate because of differing accounts as to their source, cultivation, end, and purpose.

[40] See Clapper's helpful treatment of this dynamic in Clapper, *John Wesley on Religious Affections*, pp. 121-22.

[41] Runyon, *The New Creation*, p. 165.

sionately following Christ. Wesley used a number of categories and classifications to designate the means of grace, and he included under this heading what one could label spiritual disciplines, sacraments, social outreach endeavors, and the like.[42] If God's grace can be conceived as God's 'active presence-power-influence',[43] then the manner in which it can be apprehended and received is particularly determined by Godself, and God has revealed within God's economy of salvation that God's people are to attend to God's presence through the performance of and participation in specific practices, ones that in turn lead to particular dispositions.

Broadly speaking, for Wesley the 'means of grace are means through which persons experience and respond to the loving presence of God'.[44] To quote Wesley himself, they are 'outward signs, words, or actions ordained of God, and appointed for this end – to be the *ordinary* channels whereby he might convey to men preventing, justifying, or sanctifying grace'.[45] Naturally, the use of the term 'means' can be misleading: These activities are not meant to be ends in themselves, nor are they to be mechanisms that automatically ensure God's presence in a *quid pro quo* manner. In both extremes, the focus is on the agent and one's activity rather than the object and purpose of the activity. The advocacy of the 'means of grace' therefore requires careful framing, and Wesley's nuancing of the theme is helpful.

The qualification required in Wesley's mind for a salutary understanding of the means of grace is one that attends to the Wesleyan understanding of soteriological synergy. For Wesley, the best way to describe the means of grace would be *active forms of waiting* for the divine presence.[46] On the one hand, this operative definition points to the active nature of the means of grace: Believers are to attend to their spiritual lives, to 'work out their own salvation' in such a fashion that they are not idle or lackadaisical. Wesley was keenly aware

---

[42] The benchmark study for Wesley's understanding of the means of grace continues to be Henry H. Knight, III, *The Presence of God in the Christian Life: John Wesley and the Means of Grace* (Metuchen: Scarecrow, 1992).

[43] See Heitzenrater, 'God with Us'.

[44] Knight, *The Presence of God in the Christian Life*, p. 2.

[45] Wesley, 'The Means of Grace', I, p. 381 (emphasis in the original).

[46] Wesley remarks, 'According to the decision of Holy Writ, all who desire the grace of God are to wait for it in the means which he hath ordained; in using, not in laying them aside' ('The Means of Grace', I, p. 384).

of the fact that living implies activity and performance. If time and opportunity are available, then activity is inevitably implicated as a feature of human existence. Therefore, in contradistinction to the Quietism that he came to see emerging in some of his fellowships, Wesley repeatedly made the point that the Christian life is an active life. If presented with the possibility of attending to the means of grace, one should do so not simply out of obligation or because it is something good to do but rather because attending to these is intrinsic to maintaining the vitality and dynamism required of the spiritual life within fallen conditions. Having granted the point, however, Wesley understood that this endeavoring is a kind of practiced and sustained receptivity, one that looks to something infinitely more valuable and necessary. The practice of the means of grace cannot coerce God or manipulate God into action; they do not guarantee blessing or favor. At their core, the means of grace are expressions of intentional waiting, ones that look to the possibility that God will work and move in one's life. When God does work, everything else is made possible and meaningful; without an intentional recognition of being *coram Deo* by its practitioners, the means of grace lose their rationale and so become something else in the process.

As 'active forms of waiting' for God's presence, the means of grace attend to the complexity of spiritual formation. The triune God is at the center, and this intention is vitalized by an attentiveness to one's own condition. This particular logic is at the core of what can be termed 'heart religion', a view of the Christian life in which the religious affections and holy tempers are crucially shaped through active responsiveness.[47] When believers practice the means of grace, they locate themselves in doxological space and mode; in doing so, they recognize and join God's activity of working in and transforming their lives, a work that heals and frees them from their bondage to sin and characterizes and shapes them in order that they may have the 'mind of Christ'. All of the traits listed above in terms of orthopathy and religious affections point to the way the Holy Spirit goes about shaping a holy people. The dynamic of the means

---

[47] Clapper elsewhere notes, 'We might say that a central function of all the means of grace for Wesley is the task of correctly targeting our affections on God' (Gregory S. Clapper, '*Orthokardia*: The Practical Theology of John Wesley's Heart Religion', *Quarterly Review* 10 [1990], p. 52).

of grace is clear, yet it is also a running challenge to appreciate in its many dimensions. Ultimately, what is important within this model is God's work, and so believers wait for God's self-presentation, and yet this waiting is not mindless or rote but very much intentional and directed in an active and sustained way from the human side of the dynamic. Within this synergistic interplay, the spiritual senses are awakened and the fruit of the Spirit flourish. Over time, believers 'see' and 'hear' with greater acuity and attentiveness what God is doing, and as such they increasingly mature and grow in conformity to the divine image.

4. Pentecostal Affectivity

Given the proposals by Solivan and Land as well as the Wesleyan retrieval on offer by Runyon and Clapper, what can one say about normative human affectivity in light of the task of constructing a Pentecostal moral theology?

A running theme throughout these proposals is their christological basis and form. Christ's life displays in concretized form what normative human affectivity looks like, and in turn this particular human life makes possible its imaging by others. One can speak of having the mind and heart of Christ because this life is on offer in the gospel narratives and continually proclaimed and testified to by apostolic and ecclesial witness and apprehended by the work of the Spirit. Under this heading, one could fit the varying programs above. Solivan wishes to point to Christ, particularly his incarnation, as a way of registering the concrete, active, and relational features implied by the claim that God is with us and for us in Christ. One could make similar claims with regard to Land and Wesley in that Christ provides the model of spirituality, the form of the Christian life that believers are to follow and imitate. This existential and aesthetic form of expression – a human life – suggests that nothing less than human lives are required in the process of following Christ. This remark would mean then the integration of the three 'orthos' and not simply an emphasis on the affective register. Nevertheless, poignant in Christ's life and teachings is precisely the affective dimension of living *coram Deo*. Without the linchpin of orthopathy between orthodoxy and orthopraxy, the Christian life, when perceived as a performance that takes its cue from Christ's life, is impossible to sustain integrally and genuinely.

If Christ is the basis and form for Pentecostal affectivity, then its activating and enabling force is the presence and work of the Holy Spirit. For all the value that exists in the concretization of a particular human life (as one sees in the person of Jesus), such particularity and embeddedness are potential impediments to the establishment of God's kingdom on earth because of their limits in terms of context and finitude. All the figures mentioned above would say that the Spirit is actively involved in the promotion and sustainment of normative Christian affectivity. Such work takes place within doxological intentionality. This point is especially on display in Land's depiction of Pentecostalism as a spirituality and in the Wesleyan emphasis upon the means of grace. When believers recognize their lives as existentially epicletic, when they recognize that all that they have and are and hope to be is made possible by the Spirit's presence and work, then they perform their lives in such a fashion that they themselves can be indicative – one could even say iconic – of the divine presence in the world. By sheer gratuity of the Holy Spirit, Pentecostal being-in-the-world is sacramental.[48]

However, sacramentality, as it is used in relation to a human life, implies performance, enactment, and embodiment. As Clapper remarks, 'To love God and one's neighbor, to take joy in the happiness of others, to fear the wrath of God, all imply dispositions to behave in certain ways'.[49] This feature of the logic is crucial: Normative affectivity is only compelling when on display in a human life. Affectivity is not reductively relatable as a concept or as a specified action. In a sense, it is a phenomenon that has to be witnessed, and for this reason, the Pentecostal penchant to render testimony is so crucial to Pentecostal moral theology because the practice opens up imaginative possibilities for living in the present in light of reconfigured expectations about what the triune God can, does, and will do within the economy of healing. For this reason, Pentecostals have long believed that their most effective witness to the truthful-

---

[48] Sacramentality is not a topic discussed often by Pentecostals, but it is one meriting more attention; see the promising article by Wolfgang Vondey and Chris W. Green, 'Between This and That: Reality and Sacramentality in the Pentecostal Worldview', *Journal of Pentecostal Theology* 19 (2010), pp. 265-91.

[49] Clapper, *John Wesley on Religious Affections*, p. 80.

ness and power of the gospel is a changed human life. Without the possibility of transformation, liberation, and healing (all of which could be subsumed under the headings of Pentecostal 'deliverance' and 'power')[50] and their exemplifications that make these possibilities living, walking, and talking realities, the Pentecostal message is unintelligible and so unappealing.

The holy affections could include a number of instantiations, but central to them is the affection of love. Clapper's view of the Wesleyan vision could equally apply to the Pentecostal construal; as he remarks in relation to Wesley's 'Preface' to his *Old Testament Notes*,

> Notice that love of God is the first effect of gaining knowledge of the things of God. The holy or religious tempers or affections flow from this primary affection of love of God. We will see again and again [in Wesley's work] that the love of God is the affective context in which all the other affections exist. Gratitude, awe and fear, joy, peace and all the rest seem to be somehow latent in this complex phenomenon called love.[51]

Edwards would agree with this opinion; in an echo of the quote that began this chapter, he remarks, 'But it is doubtless true ... that the essence of all true religions lies in holy love; and that in this divine affection, and an habitual disposition to it, and that light which is the foundation of it, and those things which are the fruits of it, consists the whole of religion'.[52] Early American Pentecostals, including Richard G. Spurling in *The Lost Link*, as well as William J. Seymour's reflections toward the end of the Azusa revival, pressed for similar claims.[53]

This kind of negotiation of the religious affections points to something broader worth considering. Definitionally, these holy tempers are abiding dispositions inculcated by the Holy Spirit and grounded in the love of God.[54] This recognition brings about both

---

[50] See Dale Coulter, '"Delivered by the Power of God": Toward a Pentecostal Understanding of Salvation', *International Journal of Systematic Theology* 10 (2008), pp. 447-67.

[51] Clapper, *John Wesley on Religious Affections*, p. 28.

[52] Edwards, *The Works of Jonathan Edwards*, vol. 2: *Religious Affections*, p. 107.

[53] See their treatments in Douglas Jacobsen, *Thinking in the Spirit: Theologies of the Early Pentecostal Movement* (Bloomington: Indiana University Press, 2003), pp. 52 and 79.

[54] I tend to conflate the affections and tempers in accordance with the reading of Clapper in 'John Wesley's Theology of the Heart', *Wesleyan Theological Jour-*

a certain relation (God transforming the world) on the basis of a certain rationale (because God so loved the world) in the God-cosmos dynamic, but it also beckons that one, on the basis of the God-human encounter, goes about life in a certain way (loving God and the neighbor whom God also loves). Through this synergistic interplay one is brought back to the dynamic of abiding in the triune God and actively waiting for the divine self-disclosure. Therefore, this interplay helps to negotiate the variability one finds in the concretization of these affections in Scripture. For instance, the list in Isaiah 11 (wisdom, understanding, counsel, might, knowledge, and fear of the Lord) as well as much of what one finds in the enumeration in 1 Corinthians 12 (particularly wisdom, knowledge, and faith)[55] and 13 (faith, hope, and love) would fit the workable framework of religious affections; but the catalogue of 'fruit of the Spirit' one finds in Galatians 5 is especially apropos (love, joy, peace, patience, kindness, generosity, faithfulness, gentleness, and self-control). These various gifts 'are activated by one and the same Spirit' (1 Cor. 12.11), and they mark the life that is lived and guided by the Spirit (Gal. 5.25) rather than the flesh. The Spirit prompts and makes them possible, but their intended result is a kind of life marked by the divine character, one baptized by the Spirit.[56] In oth-

---

nal 44 (2009), pp. 94-102; however, there is a controversy about the matter; see Kenneth J. Collins 'John Wesley's Topography of the Heart: Dispositions, Tempers, and Affections', *Methodist History* 36 (1998), pp. 162-75 and Maddox, 'A Change of Affections'.

[55] Of course, Pentecostals would not want to forget (and rightfully so) the rest of the items that Paul mentions, including the gifts of healing, the working of miracles, prophecy, discernment of spirits, various kinds of tongues, and interpretation of tongues. Although these would not fit the categorization of normative affectivity in neat and tidy ways, Pentecostals would undoubtedly be inclined to say that they would be marks of normative praxis among the fellowship of believers.

[56] Although the point cannot be developed here, one could make the argument that Spirit baptism within the Pentecostal fold was never about simply speaking in tongues. The experience was assumed to usher in a new modality of being-in-the-world marked by power for the purpose of witness. Frank Macchia highlights this point when he recalls that in the early literature there were a number of instances which took Rom. 5.5 to indicate that Spirit baptism is a baptism in the divine love (see Frank Macchia, 'The Kingdom and the Power: Spirit Baptism in Pentecostal and Ecumenical Perspective' in Michael Welker (ed.), *The Work of the Spirit: Pneumatology and Pentecostalism* [Grand Rapids: Eerdmans, 2006], pp. 119-20, as well as his book *Baptized in the Spirit: A Global Pentecostal Theology* [Grand Rapids: Zondervan, 2006], chapter 6). If this earlier understanding is to be retrieved, then its emphases change the overall understanding of Spirit bap-

er words, this would be a form of life one could denominate as existentially epicletic. As long as such a pneumatic characterization is at work in which the community of the faithful are actively being shaped by the Spirit to be Christ-like, then the specification of gifts and fruit is not as important as their embodiment. The point of the religious affections for Pentecostals is that through them the presence and power of God are on display through human beings. The particularity and concretization involved in seeing one with the mind and heart of Christ is a vital step for the awakening of sensory and imaginative construals of what God's kingdom is and can be like, both now and in the eschaton.

5. Looking Ahead to Another Model

As this chapter has proposed, the notion of normativity within the affective life presents a number of possibilities for Pentecostals in light of the constructive task related to moral theology within their particular Christian subtradition. The vision is largely one 'from above to below' in that the religious affections tend to point to the work of the Spirit in conforming the epicletic community to the shape of Christ's life. They dispositionally alter the faithful, and the fitting response to 'suffering' such pneumatic conditioning is to live into these affections so that they can flourish and be on display as witnesses of the mighty presence and work of the triune God.

Nevertheless, one wonders if the synergistic indeterminacy that has been a running motif of this work through its dual foci of 'abiding' and 'waiting' is adequately considered through a treatment of the religious affections. In other words, is there not a model available that can move 'from below to above', not in the sense of saying that humans can aspire to God apart from God but as a way of tak-

---

tism dramatically for current-day Pentecostals: The experience is not so much to be associated with a criterion of a religious phenomenon (namely tongues) but rather as pointing to the awakening and cultivation of what has been alluded to in this monograph as the 'Pentecostal worldview' or the 'Pentecostal way of life'. In other words, Spirit baptism is appropriately tied to the phenomenon of Spirit living, and the latter has a way of being eclipsed by the former when the former is strictly associated with glossolalia generally and initial evidence thinking particularly. For a treatment of this topic and its surrounding epistemic constraints within the framework of the movement known as 'canonical theism', see Daniel Castelo, 'Canonical Theism as Ecclesial and Ecumenical Resource', *Pneuma* 33 (2011), pp. 370-89.

ing into account a resilient estimation of a doctrine of creation so that human flourishing is somehow related to participating and cultivating the *imago Dei*? A model of this kind does exist, and Christians have made good use of it over the centuries. The model is virtue theory, and it will be considered at length in the chapter that follows.

3

HABITUATING THE PRACTICE-ORIENTATIONS OF ABIDING AND WAITING

As noted in the previous chapter, the Christian affections are often described as pneumatically cultivated dispositions that shape the believer. A scriptural passage that promotes this logic is Rom. 5.5, 'And hope does not disappoint us, because God's love has been poured into our hearts through the Holy Spirit that has been given to us'. The movement within the affections is significantly accented 'from above to below' in that it emphasizes what the triune God does in believers' hearts to shape and mold them into the likeness of Christ. Such accentuation need not diminish the importance of inhabiting and embodying these affections since they would mean nothing apart from their instantiation as witnesses to God's ongoing work of healing and repair. Nevertheless, the emphasis is clear, and it is one that Pentecostals naturally find compelling given their traditional inclination to believe that the most significant change that can take place in a person's life stems from the altar encounter with the triune God.[1]

Since they are dispositional in orientation, the affections are sometimes also referred to as virtues, or at least the two categories are used interchangeably by some. For instance, Don Saliers (the *Doktorvater* of both Land and Clapper) could say the following in a seminal article years ago: 'The Christian moral life is the embodi-

---

[1] Dale Coulter makes the connection between encounter and affectivity within Pentecostalism in, Dale Coulter, 'Pentecostalism, Mysticism, and Renewal Methodologies', *Pneuma* 33 (2011), pp. 1-4.

ment of those affections and virtues which are intentional orientation of existence in Jesus Christ' as well as 'Affections and virtues
grounded in the saving mystery of Christ constitute a way of being
moral'.[2] Clapper also follows this logic in his reading of Wesley:
'The dispositional nature of the affections makes them more like
virtues than feelings'.[3] Additionally, D. Stephen Long concludes his
work on Wesley's moral theology with an appendix in which he interchangeably negotiates both tempers and virtues.[4] This reading of
Wesley's usage of terms, shared by both Clapper and Long, is important because on simply textual evidence, one can make the case
that John Wesley was a eudemonist.[5]

As interchangeable as the two models are, they are nevertheless
distinguishable in important ways. If the affections thrive within a
logic of moving 'from above to below', the virtues could suggest
the complementary notion, of moving 'from below to above'. Of
course, simply the admission of this logic is counterintuitive for
some Pentecostals given a hyperextended Protestant aversion toward works-righteousness that many Pentecostals naturally assume.
If one can suspend this well-established concern and hermeneutic
temporarily, one could possibly grant the legitimacy of the claim
that human action does matter for the preservation and flourishing
of God's work within the epicletic community. Essentially, this emphasis is the other side of the ongoing theme in the present work,
one that heightens the synergistic indeterminacy of Pentecostal being-in-the-world through the emphases of abiding and waiting.

This focus on human participation is itself biblical, for it can be
found in a number of passages that are often appealed to in moral
theology. One of Wesley's running scriptural warrants for his vision

---

[2] Don E. Saliers, 'Liturgy and Ethics: Some New Beginnings', *Journal of Religious Ethics* 7 (1979), p. 179.

[3] Clapper, *John Wesley on Religious Affections*, p. 85.

[4] D. Stephen Long, *John Wesley's Moral Theology: The Quest for God and Goodness*
(Nashville: Kingswood, 2005), pp. 245-47.

[5] To take but one example, in Wesley's letter of 19 July 1731 to 'Aspasia'
(Mary Pendarves), Wesley clearly employs a eudemonistic framework in light of
the complementarity of affections and virtues in the Christian life: 'I was made to
be happy: to be happy I must love God; in proportion to my love of whom my
happiness must increase. To love God I must be like him, holy as He is holy;
which implies both the being pure from vicious and foolish passions and the
being confirmed in those virtuous and rational affections which God comprises
in the word "charity"' (*The Letters of the Rev. John* Wesley [8 vols.; ed. John Telford;
Epworth: London: 1931], I, pp. 92-93).

of Christian perfection was Phil. 2.12, 'Work out your own salvation with fear and trembling'.[6] Another prominent passage along these lines is 2 Pet. 1.4-5, 'Thus he has given us, through these things, his precious and very great promises, so that through them you may escape from the corruption that is in the world because of lust, and may become participants of the divine nature. For this very reason, you must make every effort to support your faith with goodness'. Throughout the scriptural testimony and inherent to Christian antiquity are the dual movements of 'from above to below' and 'from below to above'. Protestantism has made it especially difficult to see the scriptural justification for the latter, but the two movements are available and necessary for a vital and attentive vision of moral theology, and whereas the affections attend to the former in important ways, the virtues can attend to the latter.

The importance of virtue theory comes through via the recognition of the following difficulty. If the accentuation falls heavily on the movement 'from above to below', what to make of human agency and activity? Are these simply ancillary, or do they naturally follow from the 'springs' that are the affections? Does human activity have no bearing on the way humans are continually and vitally disposed and characterized over time? For those traditions that wish to emphasize God's glory and God's preeminence at the potential expense of human activity, the worry is repeatedly registered that we cannot make ourselves holy for this would be the culmination of idolatry. And yet, at various moments within the biblical testimony, hearers and readers are called to 'sanctify themselves'. The divine imperative runs through the testaments, both in the Levitical law and in the Sermon on the Mount. If the divine imperative is a mark of God's self-disclosing will for God's people, then is the command simply a perfunctory 'do this because you should' notion or does it somehow play an integral role, one of characterizing a people unto God-likeness?

The virtues, as represented in Aristotle and his qualified employment for Christian purposes by Aquinas, display a theory of human action that can attend to this quandary. In fact, the difficulty itself is not simply related to the way one negotiates the biblical ma-

---

[6] The synergistic indeterminacy is present here as well since Paul continues in the next verse, 'for it is God who is at work in you, enabling you both to will and to work for his good pleasure'.

terials but also pertinent to the way ethical thinking has shifted within Western intellectual history. This intellectual heritage not only makes the divine imperative so difficult to appreciate in the contemporary context but it also complicates the possibility of moral speech more generally. For this reason and many more, an Aristotelian revival of sorts has taken place both within the secular and Christian academy.[7]

1. The Need for an Alternative

Generally, this re-appropriation of Aristotle by the academy relates to the bankruptcy that has become clearer surrounding the project of modernity. Gradually, contemporary thinkers have come to acknowledge the sheer embeddedness of human existence and how such contextual particularities relate to the rituals and customs that humans use to form and constitute their self-identity and purpose. Christian thinkers in particular have found these gestures important, and they have gone on to employ the virtues alongside other categories such as 'narratives', 'traditions', and (to recall one of the themes of Chapter 1) 'practices'. In both cases, a running recognition has emerged that moral inquiry within the conventional paradigms and thought forms associated with late modernity are impoverished resources for aiding people in negotiating such basic considerations as the nature of the good life, happiness, and meaningfulness.

One example common to all within contemporary Western society should suggest the need for an alternative model within ethical enquiry. Many today find moral matters to be simply ones related to 'catch-22' situations where what one decides to do is the focus in the midst of anguishing alternatives. The prevalent question within this model of obligation is 'What should I do?' It focuses on moral quandaries and places an exorbitant amount of pressure on the individual to make the 'right choice' in the midst of less than felicitous circumstances.[8] Moral debate today is often enshrined within

---

[7] For a helpful summary of the various arguments used against and for virtue theory within Christian ethical reflection, see Joseph J. Kotva, Jr, *The Christian Case for Virtue Ethics* (Washington, DC: Georgetown University Press, 1996).

[8] Notice how the running theme of an ethics of obligation is duty; this inclination is largely due to the influence of Kant. In his typically helpful fashion,

this model, making the topic of morality appear contentious, divisive, and so threatening. If the 'right' choice is to be made, then one has to operate from (or at least implicitly assume) some principle or authority by which to determine whether something is 'right' or 'wrong'. And yet, it is widely assumed within the contemporary moral climate in the West that there is no way to adjudicate definitively between competing rival authorities or premises in moral deliberation. This reality makes public discourse in all things moral not only interminable but it also suggests, or at least gives the appearance of, 'a disquieting private arbitrariness'.[9] Within this scenario is the potential conflation of personal preferences with particular adherence to authorities of moral evaluation, and such equivalence can lead to a prevalent and often implicitly assumed understanding or perspective called 'emotivism'. According to MacIntyre, 'Emotivism is the doctrine that all evaluative judgments and more specifically all moral judgments are *nothing but* expressions of preference, expressions of attitude or feeling, insofar as they are moral or evaluative in character'.[10]

In light of this state of affairs, several questions are worth asking. Is the default of the self and one's tastes and preferences sufficient to narrate a meaningful life? Is the portrayal of the self as the ultimate authority helpful and compelling for charting a happy and good life? Does this strategy not in fact assume a disengaged and anonymous agent as well as a 'placeless place' for a context? Is this kind of privileging really not a reduction of what it means to be human, and does it not subscribe to a myopic fantasy of sorts regarding the ways humans are shaped and forged both by the cultural inheritance they receive as well as by the actions and choices they make over time?

The resurgence in virtue theory recognizes both the features of the contemporary moral landscape in late modernity as well as many of its limits highlighted by the questions above and in turn provides alternatives within such vacuums. Broadly stated, virtue

---

Servais Pinckaers is instructive here: 'Kant gives priority to duty over love in his interpretation of the first commandment of God. For Kant this commandment imposes a duty and not a sentiment' (Servais Pinckaers, *Morality: The Catholic View* [South Bend, IN: St. Augustine's, 2001], p. 67). This move contributed to the diminishment of happiness as a legitimate end in moral reflection.

[9] MacIntyre, *After Virtue*, p. 8.

[10] MacIntyre, *After Virtue*, pp. 11-12 (emphasis in original).

theory is appealing because it assumes a 'morality of happiness' rather than a 'morality of obligation', and the differences between both approaches are drastic. A morality of happiness emphasizes that the goal of a human life is not simply to be consistent with one's principles or tastes but to be happy, the latter denoting not so much a fleeting emotion of jubilation but rather a perduring reality that points to a normative account of human flourishing, purposefulness, and generativity. Unlike a morality of obligation, a morality of happiness assumes that acts are determinative for morality because they are constitutive and formative of the self; as one recent commentator has remarked about the morality of happiness, 'Rules that we follow not only point us toward that further goal, but are very participation in that goal, rather than simply a means to some extrinsically related end'.[11] Instead of instrumentalizing action and so making it tangential, a morality of happiness places a premium on performance, on enacting and inhabiting the good over time and with practice. In this model, people are allowed 'to get it wrong' as doing so is part of learning the different aspects of the good. The contexts of action are not so much a-contextual moments of decision-making but indications of the way a person has been shaped and formed over time on the basis of a specific account of the good. This de-privileging of quandaries in turn helps show how all of one's life has a moral tenor to it and not simply those infelicitous (and often unlikely) hypotheticals. Put generally, a morality of happiness emphasizes the 'art of living' whereas a morality of obligation casts a methodological shadow of logic, deduction, and Euclidian reasoning upon the ethical task itself.

Christians for centuries have recognized the value of virtue ethics and its possible links with the Christian life. To be a Christian, it has been assumed, is to lead a certain kind of life. Another way of phrasing the matter is that Christian existence pivots on both an encounter with the triune God and a calling to follow this God. Christians are to have the mind of Christ and to have the first-fruits of the kingdom resplendent for all to see, but they have consistently acknowledged that 'being salt and light' does not simply happen in an instant but that this command and call beckon intentional, steady, and ongoing performance. A Christian appropriation of the

---

[11] William C. Mattison, III, *Introducing Moral Theology: True Happiness and the Virtues* (Grand Rapids: Brazos, 2008), p. 35.

virtues integrates many of these concerns because a teleological (as distinguished from a deontological) framing allows for God to be the 'end' or 'purpose' of existence. In the Christian sense, the created order has come from God and is returning to God, and it is in God that the creation finds its true meaning because this participatory state is one in which the creation can truly be said to live and flourish (and so, be happy). Augustine expressed the matter fittingly: 'How then am I to seek you, Lord? When I seek you, my God, what I am seeking is a life of happiness. Let me seek you that my soul may live, for as my body draws its life from my soul, so does my soul draw its life from you'.[12]

Despite this longstanding tradition within Christian reflection, Pentecostals have rarely engaged virtue theory.[13] The difficulty, perhaps, stems from the way that virtue theory promotes a certain kind of activism that is stereotyped as strategies toward 'self-improvement'. This caricature, however, fails to recognize the embedded nature of human living. All living assumes some kind of norm, so each person is 'self-improving' or 'self-degenerating' according to some operative norm just simply by being. In other words, people do not choose to be moral; they already are by being and acting in the world; therefore, the pressing challenge is more fittingly described as identifying the morality one already assumes to guide one's actions (rather than choosing to be moral in the first place) and in turn evaluating that assumed morality in relation to the good one assumes for one's life. Admittedly, the virtues in one sense can emphasize a 'from below to above' vantage point,[14] but that angle is quite helpful in balancing the 'from above to below' perspective that Pentecostals privilege. This particular resonance of virtue theory would help *sustain* 'Pentecostal being-in-the-world', a need that is sorely pressing for the viability of Pentecostal identity across time. In a sense, Pentecostals need a moral vision that can sustain them

---

[12] Augustine, *Confessions*, X (trans. Maria Boulding; New York: Vintage, 1997).

[13] One notable exception is Paul W. Lewis, 'A Pneumatological Approach to Virtue Ethics', *Asian Journal of Pentecostal Studies* 1 (1998), pp. 42-61. Unfortunately, one of the limits of Lewis' article is its oversight of the Thomistic tradition; the present chapter will carry on a conversation with this important representation of virtue theory within Christian moral reflection as a way to orient Pentecostals in their moral vision.

[14] Aquinas' account is much more complex than this single movement; more will be said regarding this point below.

in 'ordinary' time, one that is informed but nevertheless distinct from formal altar encounters of transformation. The necessary admission would be that not simply a revivalist setting but the entire modality of being *coram Deo* is potentially capable of transformative and life-altering implications for the shaping of the epicletic community across generations.

What follows is a survey of virtue theory and its Christian reconfiguration so that the possibilities for this model within moral theology can become clearer. Such an endeavor will include an exploration of Aristotle's *Nicomachean Ethics* as well as Aquinas' continuity with and divergence from this project in the *Summa theologiae*. Particularly important in the consideration of Aquinas is the synergistic interplay between divine and human activity, one that not only points to corollaries with the model of the religious affections but also with the overarching metaphor of epicletic existence that the present work has sustained. Finally, some constructive considerations will be leveled in order to relate the importance that Christian virtue theory could play in the role and ongoing negotiation of Pentecostal being-in-the-world.

2. Beginning with Aristotle

Aristotle initiates his classic work on ethics with a very telling remark: 'Every craft and every line of inquiry, and likewise every action and decision, seems to seek some good'.[15] In other words, people pursue activities and behave in certain ways because they assume that such exertions are worthwhile. Aristotle goes on to ask, 'What is the highest of all the goods achievable in action?'[16] His answer is that this highest of all goods is 'happiness' or *eudaimonia*. Now Aristotle is willing to admit that people define happiness in a variety of ways, but he at least wishes to secure conceptually the category itself before providing a normative vision for what it could be. The important move here is to frame human action in a particular way, namely as seeking goods related to particular actions themselves; as examples, medicine would pursue one good, boatbuilding another, household management another, and so forth.

---

[15] Aristotle, *Nicomachean Ethics*, I.1 (trans. Terence Irwin; Indianapolis: Hackett, 2nd edn, 1999).
[16] Aristotle, *Nicomachean Ethics*, I.4.

The Philosopher moves from negotiating human action to considering anthropology more generally. Aristotle recognizes that the multiplicity of goods as well as the potential abstraction surrounding the notion of happiness both require something more concretely stated about human beings. Essentially, Aristotle poses the question of what is the proper function of human existence. Just as a flautist and a sculptor pursue goods through their activity in light of their particular roles, an analogue regarding humans more generally applies in Aristotle's view. The question simply put is: Do human beings themselves have a proper and fitting function, one that they can grow into over time and through training so as to realize a good life? Aristotle answers the question in the affirmative and offers the following: 'For the function of a harpist is to play the harp, and the function of a good harpist is to play it well. Moreover, we take the human function to be a certain kind of life, and take this life to be activity and actions of the soul that involve reason; hence the function of the excellent man is to do this well and finely'.[17]

This interplay between the soul's activities and reason is precisely facilitated, refined, and prompted toward excellence through the inculcation of the virtues. Aristotle defines the virtues at varying points as 'states' or 'conditions' that are praiseworthy and compatible with the human condition so that they can constitute a kind of 'second nature'. Human beings are not born with the virtues, but they can acquire them in analogous ways to how crafts are acquired: 'We become builders ... by building, and we become harpists by playing the harp. Similarly, then, we become just by doing just actions, temperate by doing temperate actions, brave by doing brave actions'.[18] Essentially, Aristotle considers the self as a mass of potential that can be honed and cultivated so as to arrive at its proper functioning. The virtues then represent those states, conditions, or 'habits'[19] that can be acquired over time and through ongoing intentionality that in turn lead to human flourishing, that is, *eudaimonia*.

---

[17] Aristotle, *Nicomachean Ethics*, I.7.

[18] Aristotle, *Nicomachean Ethics*, II.1.

[19] The rendering of 'habit' for the Latin *habitus* can be problematic; see the helpful article by Servais Pinckaers, 'Virtue is not a Habit', *Cross Currents* 12 (1962), pp. 65-81.

Aristotle's account is exceedingly complex, and a summary section here cannot explore its many dimensions, but a few observations are in order for the project at hand.

First, one can detect within Aristotle a logic of human characterization that is at its basis a form of circular reasoning. This quality of circularity is not due to a flawed conceptual scheme, for it arises out of inductive observations of how humans are shaped over time. On the one hand, to inhabit any of the virtues, one must will and desire to start mimicking and copying an exemplar of the virtue in question. One needs a model to follow so that one can start over time to learn through an apprenticeship of sorts what all is involved in embodying and sustaining a specific virtue. Such intentional activity will come to shape the agent so that the virtue in question will begin to mark her character. The virtue-seeker will move from being an imitator of a virtuous exemplar to a virtuous person herself over time. At one point, Aristotle fleshes out other features of this logic. He remarks that virtuous actions are not simply ones that are in accord with virtue but they have to emit from a practitioner who 1) intentionally and knowingly pursues virtuous actions, 2) does so without any ulterior motive, and 3) emits the virtue from a firm and unchanging state.[20] With these points in consideration, the circularity presses the following question: Do only virtuous people perform virtuous actions or do virtuous actions make virtuous people? The answer, of course, is doubly affirmative.[21] The conceptual indeterminacy at play here is appropriate in that characterization through habituation is often recognized fully only *post factum*. It may be difficult to know oneself exceedingly and fittingly throughout this entire process, but such moments of recognitional subsequence (by others and the self) mark the human experience of formation. Although this observation regarding hindsight is occasionally present in Aristotle, the implicit understanding is that the pursuer of happiness is teleologically directed (that is, forward-looking).

Second, Aristotle admits that the virtuous life is a difficult one because it beckons an ongoing detection and resistance of extremes and so the inhabitation of the 'intermediate condition'. He notes,

---

[20] See Aristotle, *Nicomachean Ethics*, II.4.

[21] The *Catechism of the Catholic Church* follows this logic and states the matter quite compellingly: 'The moral virtues are acquired by human effort. They are the *fruit and seed* of morally good acts' (1804, emphasis added).

'That is why it is also hard work to be excellent. For in each case it is hard work to find the intermediate ... getting angry, or giving and spending money, is easy and everyone can do it; but doing it to the right person, in the right amount, at the right time, for the right end, and in the right way is no longer easy, nor can everyone do it. Hence doing these things well is rare, praiseworthy, and fine'.[22] Every virtue rests within the spectrum of two extremes, one of deficiency and one of excess. To take but one example, bravery rests between cowardice and rashness; the excesses are easy to enact, but the mean, the virtue of bravery, is difficult to sustain.[23] Nevertheless their difficulty makes the virtues all the more praiseworthy and desirable since the excesses are not simply easier but also widely esteemed as deplorable. Cowardly and rash people are not ideal types; they are generally not understood as models for imitation. For all the ambiguity and tensions surrounding moral inquiry today, it is fascinating how the vices Aristotle has in mind are widely held as unbecoming to a good life.

Finally, one of the most normative claims Aristotle makes is both simple and yet perhaps counter-intuitive for many of his readers: The virtuous life *is* the happy life. The claim makes sense on many levels, but Aristotle is aware that it is a difficult argument to sustain given the sundry elements constitutive of human experience. Some would say that the happy life would be the life of amusement or relaxation, and these naysayers could sound out a number of apparent examples to prove the point. But here is where Aristotle's normative anthropology comes through: If the ideal, flourishing, mature human life (that is, the one that is functioning well on the basis of an account that states specifically what this is) is the one marked by the virtues (and it appears as such, given the general deplorability associated with the vices and the praiseworthiness of the virtues), then it only naturally follows that activities consonant with this ideal would lead to happiness. The logic is a movement from a normative account of human nature to a normative account of human action; it would only make sense that the ideal exemplification of a human life would dictate what the ideal, proper, meaningful, and so happy enactment of that life would be.

---

[22] Aristotle, *Nicomachean Ethics*, II.9.
[23] See Aristotle's discussion in *Nicomachean Ethics*, II.8.

These and many other points in the *Nicomachean Ethics* were picked up in a qualified sense by Thomas Aquinas' cathedral-like work, one which happens to be, among many things, one of the great resources from Christian antiquity for constructive moral theology today.

3. Continuing with Aquinas

A radical shift and reorientation within Roman Catholic moral theology came about at Vatican II with its 'Decree on Priestly Training'; therein, the field of moral theology is addressed: 'Special care must be given to the perfecting of moral theology. Its scientific exposition, nourished more on the teaching of the Bible, should shed light on the loftiness of the calling of the faithful in Christ and the obligation that is theirs of bearing fruit in charity for the life of the world'.[24] In particular, a distancing from the manualist and casuist traditions of moral reflection is envisioned. Given this charge, the aid of Thomas Aquinas has been employed by many Roman Catholics in order to heed this call for reform.

Why Thomas? His is a realist moral theology, one that 'views the human person as set between God and God'.[25] The *exitus-reditus* scheme he employs facilitates an integrationist vision in which moral theology is placed within *sacra doctrina*; as Cessario relates, 'Aquinas's method aims to situate every question related to our achieving perfect happiness within a full theological context, with the result that only pedagogical considerations warrant distinguishing between moral and dogmatic theology'.[26] Therefore, moral considerations are not considered ancillary or tangential to the theological task in Thomas' mind but very much an integral feature of what it means to participate and be conformed to Christ.

Thomas promotes his views on moral theology within the *Secunda Pars* of the *Summa Theologiae*, and as it is obvious from the beginnings of this section, his work is indebted significantly to Aristotle's methodological intuitions. These include a valorization of ends for understanding purpose and meaningfulness, an appreciation of the

---

24 *Optatam totius*, 16.
25 Romanus Cessario, *Introduction to Moral Theology* (Washington, DC: Catholic University of America Press, 2001), p. xix.
26 Cessario, *Introduction to Moral Theology*, p. 9.

goal of human life as happiness, and an employment of virtue theory for understanding growth in perfection. Thomas continues with the tradition of emphasizing the cardinal virtues as well as developing a theory of action. In all these features, Thomas draws significantly from Aristotle's patterns of thinking and elaboration.

With such convergences, one may wonder about the role of the Christian faith in all of this development. What does the Christian account of human purposes and ends offer to the discussion that in turn has to change or alter Aristotle's reflections? In other words, what makes Aquinas' vision distinctly Christian? These are important questions, yet their exploration does not result in simplistic answers; it is not enough to say that Aquinas 'baptized' or 'Christianized' Aristotle, for that cheapens the legitimacy of Aquinas' project on its own terms. Aquinas, as all do, employed a conceptual framework that was available to him, and he did so as a means of applying its logic for purposes of narrating and negotiating both the depths and riches of the Christian vision of how things are.[27] Therefore, Aquinas' vision is distinctly Christian, and claims to the contrary are shortsighted and ungenerous.[28]

To begin, one can look to the prologue of the *Prima Secundae*: 'Now that we have treated of the exemplar, *i.e.*, God, and of those things which came forth from the power of God in accordance with His will; it remains for us to treat of His image, *i.e.*, man, inasmuch as he too is the principle of his actions, as having free-will and control of his actions'.[29] The claim suggests that speaking of humanity as God's image requires an account that can address *all* humans, Christian and non-Christian alike, while at the same time offering such a vision in a distinctly Christian way, one that

---

[27] Aquinas addresses the point with regard to the interplay of *sacra doctrina* and the philosophers: 'But sacred doctrine makes use even of human reason, not, indeed, to prove faith ... but to make clear other things that are put forward in this doctrine. Since therefore grace does not destroy nature, but perfects it, natural reason should minister to faith as the natural bent of the will ministers to charity ... Hence sacred doctrine makes use also of the authority of philosophers in those questions in which they were able to know the truth by natural reason' (*ST*, I, q.1, a.8, r.2); the translation of the *Summa theologiae* (hereafter *ST*) used herein is the one by the Fathers of the English Dominican Province (Allen: Christian Classics, 1948).

[28] One direct treatment of this line of inquiry can be found in Servais Pinckaers, *The Sources of Christian Ethics* (Washington, DC: Catholic University of America Press, 1995), chapter 7.

[29] *ST*, I-II, prologue.

acknowledges its proposals as within the framing of *sacra doctrina*,[30] as an endeavoring that conceives itself outright as work undertaken within the *exitus-reditus* framework of being between God and God; as such, this reflection on morality is made possible and propelled by God's self-presentation.[31]

By way of localization, one ought to recognize that Thomas' proposals do not represent a modernist account that seeks to be generalizable to all people, at all times, in all places; rather, it is a distinct movement from a particular standpoint to narrate 'all that is'. Epistemically then one may have to reorient oneself in order to grasp the intent of Aquinas. The move is self-consciously located within the economy of grace, within the God-enabled possibility of human reasoning and reflection. Secondly, this particular vantage-point suggests that all that is comes from God and is returning to God. This acknowledgement would mean that as they reason and flourish, human beings resemble, reflect, and are disposed to God in certain ways. In other words, Aquinas would admit that there is a category such as the 'virtuous pagan'. The possibility of such a person, however, does not rest on the merits of being a pagan but rather on the source, purpose, and end of humans generally and the role virtue can play in human flourishing particularly. In one sense, this person's virtue is truly virtue, but in another sense, it is (whether admitted or not by the person in question) a God-inflected instantiation of goodness that is at the same time not enough to reach one's ultimate end. In other words, Aquinas negotiates a double aspect to human ends: one natural and one supernatural.[32]

Take, for instance, the transition in Aquinas from the cardinal to the theological virtues. Aquinas recognizes that humanity's happi-

---

[30] For instance, Thomas remarks in terms of the unity of sacred science: 'Sacred doctrine does not treat of God and creatures equally, but of God primarily; and of creatures only so far as they are referable to God as their beginning or end' (*ST*, I, q.1, a.3, r.1).

[31] These considerations are significantly on display by the very ordering of the *Summa* into its three parts as well as the content of its beginning, which is a consideration of the shape and nature of *sacra doctrina*.

[32] Naturally, both complexity and ambiguity surround these claims as they are made by Thomas. Obviously, the supernatural does not do away with the natural (as the quotes below will show), but Thomas wishes to maintain the integrity of the natural even as he elaborates the supernatural. A way forward is to negotiate these claims in terms of different 'aspects' and 'proximities'. One helpful reading is found in Jean Porter, *The Recovery of Virtue: The Relevance of Aquinas for Christian Ethics* (Louisville: Westminster John Knox, 1990), pp. 63-68.

ness is twofold: in proportion to one's human nature according to one's natural principles and another 'surpassing man's nature ... which man can obtain by the power of God alone, by a kind of participation in the Godhead'.[33] Thomas continues: 'And because such happiness surpasses the capacity of human nature, man's natural principles which enable him to act well according to his capacity, do not suffice to direct man to this same happiness'.[34] As one can see, Aquinas does allow for a happiness that is tied to one's natural rational capacities, a kind of happiness that is fitting for proper human functioning; at the same time, Aquinas will grant that 'God is the last end of man and all other things ... For man and other rational creatures attain to their last end by knowing and loving God'.[35] Some may not find this distinction compelling, but it is one that Aquinas grants because of a commitment to the possibility that proper human functioning is available in some sense to those who hone their natural capacities because of the 'first perfection' associated with being created in the *imago Dei*; it stems from a conviction to see the goodness of creation even after the fall.[36]

The importance of this vision for the present study is that it is a theological account of human flourishing that takes seriously the movement 'from below to above', so to speak, again not as an a-theological schematization but very much one that can be said to be thoroughly Christian in that it depicts God as font of both the natural and the evangelical law.[37] So to return to the example of the virtuous pagan, whether this person recognizes it or not, the virtue she

---

[33] *ST*, I-II, q.62, a.1.

[34] *ST*, I-II, q.62, a.1.

[35] *ST*, I-II, q.1, a.8.

[36] Edgardo A. Colón-Emeric draws this point about Aquinas in contradistinction to Wesley's orientation; see Edgardo A. Colón-Emeric *Wesley, Aquinas and Christian Perfection: An Ecumenical Dialogue* (Waco: Baylor University Press, 2009), p. 150.

[37] Obviously, some difficulties present themselves when one uses these categories, but there is some force to their reach in that they operate from an expansive account of creation that in some sense is necessary for an account of the traditional transcendentals. Cessario notes along these lines, 'Not only does natural law reveal the imprint of the *imago Dei*, but also that the voluntary character of human activity manifests the human person's analogical participation in that divine nature wherein knowing the good and willing the truth are necessarily coincident. A pattern of holiness is established at the very origins of human action. The more the rational creature chooses virtuously, the more he or she images God who is the cause of all voluntary movements' (Cessario, *Introduction to Moral Theology*, p. 101).

has, to the extent that it truly is virtue, is God-generated and God-directed in a very particular sense since she herself is one of God's creatures who is ultimately created to worship and participate in God, the *summum bonum*. One can affirm that this person demonstrates a species of the divine imprint when she operates from that stable and abiding disposition that marks her virtuous character. In this sense, the God of Christian confession, as the ultimate good, is not simply portrayed as the good of only Christians but the good of all creation. When truth, goodness, and beauty display themselves throughout the creation, they do so as indicators of their divine origin and end.

The admission suggests that the life of virtue and the life of holiness are, in a certain sense, of a piece because they both point to (albeit under different aspects) the perfection of human beings.[38] As Livio Melina notes of the *Catechism of the Catholic Church*, 'Holiness, which is identified by the *Catechism* as a universal vocation and as a response to the desire for happiness, is thus also presented as the truth of the human person'.[39] As such, the Christian saint is not simply constituted as such by a supernatural work of the Holy Spirit but also by attending to a kind of self-characterization that even certain pagans manage in a way with the proper exercise of one's natural capacities. This move is important because *the natural is not incidental to the vision of the Christian life*. In no sense are Christians exempt from honing their natural capacities; quite the contrary, if they fail to do so, in an important sense they deviate from the divine character, thereby providing impediments to their appreciation and apprehension of the good.[40] Logically persistent within the notion

---

[38] *Veritatis splendor* suggests as much when it assumes an 'intrinsic and unbreakable bond between faith and morality' (4).

[39] Livio Melina, *Sharing in Christ's Virtues: For a Renewal of Moral Theology in Light of* Veritatis Splendor (Washington, DC: Catholic University of America Press, 2001), p. 175.

[40] In making these points, I am not suggesting that a life of moral virtue somehow makes one sufficiently capable or worthily acceptable for the operation of divine grace since the latter depends solely on the divine gratuity; what I am claiming is that the life of moral virtue and the life of 'supernatural virtue' (that is, the kind that is infused by God) are not incidental to one another in that they both come from, reflect, and are directed to God, even if under different aspects. For this reason, moving 'from below to above' is still operative, valuable, and (I would say) necessary in any depiction of Christian moral formation, even ones that have the proclivity to emphasize in varying degrees and forms the movement 'from above to below'.

of 'grace perfecting nature' is that nature is capable of flourishing in a certain fitting and proper way.[41]

Of course, Thomas makes room for both considerations, that is 'above' and 'below' features of human characterization; the former is developed largely within the rubric of the theological virtues and the gifts and fruit of the Holy Spirit. An impressive feature of Thomas' approach is that he negotiates habituation by moving from the cardinal to the theological virtues in the *Prima Secundae* only to begin the *Secunda Secundae* with the theological virtues so as to deal *subsequently* with an extended account of the cardinal virtues once again. This two-pronged approach to Christian virtue theory within the *Secunda Pars* is indicative of Thomas' broader commitments to extend the logic of both nature and grace, of humanity's rational capacities and spiritual, God-enabled possibilities. In other words, his project wishes to attend to the many aspects of what it means for humans – creatures who are created by and for God – to live and flourish.

4. Why Pentecostals Need the Virtues

For all the gravitas that virtue theory has in terms of its history and influence upon Christian moral reflection, why should Pentecostals care? Would not a proposal for virtue ethics within Pentecostalism be an artificial imposition, one with little by way of convergence? Several claims could be put forward in light of these likely concerns.

As noted above, the revivalist model of religious experience, one that American Pentecostals have so persistently imbibed, has its limits in terms of moral formation. The altar experience, as powerful as it can be, is simply that: an experience. By their very nature, religious experiences come and go, and their implications and consequences (including their 'fruit') may or may not follow in due course. The religious affections, in that they were heralded by revivalists like Jonathan Edwards and John Wesley, work within revivalist contexts, and so this framework is most natural for Pentecostals to appreciate and foster. However, traditional forms of revivalism are not only waning or being reconfigured on the Ameri-

---

[41] The *Catechism of the Catholic Church* cites Gregory of Nyssa to make a vital point: 'The goal of a virtuous life is to become like God' (1803).

can scene among Pentecostals but the longstanding forms also potentially shortchange the experience of quotidian living. A human life is not simply marked by 'crisis moments' of encounter; it is also marked by the peaks and valleys of 'ordinary time'. For this reason, another model, one that can complement the religious affections, would be helpful. Such a model could give an account of living into the implications of altar encounters, and in doing so, it could give a more robust and self-aware exploration of what it means to lead a Spirit-bearing life in the world.

Related to this need, the virtues may be a way of opening the traditional Pentecostal purview of the Spirit's work within creation, and such a venue could be promising for constructive moral reflection by Pentecostals. The notion of subsequence has been keen for Pentecostals, as it works within a specific Lukan understanding of Spirit-outpouring that not only secures Spirit baptism as Pentecostals have traditionally understood it but also revivalist conventionalities more generally. But, as John Levison has recently noted, pneumatology is significantly inflected by the starting point one chooses:

> If one begins to construct a pneumatology with the book of Acts, particularly the story of Pentecost, then speaking in (other) tongues or dreams and visions may become the quintessential expression of the spirit's effects. If, however, one begins with the servant figure of Isaiah 42.1-6, then the quintessential expression of the spirit's effects is universal justice for aliens and foreigners. If one begins with the story of Bezalel, then the quintessential expression of the spirit's effects is an expansion of skills that have been cultivated in a lifelong pursuit of excellence.[42]

What Levison has managed to do is to expand the pneumatological conversation so that it moves beyond the Lukan and Pauline considerations of subsequence to the tensions related across the two biblical testaments more broadly. As Frank Macchia notes of Levi-

---

[42] John R. Levison, '*Filled with the Spirit*: A Conversation with Pentecostal and Charismatic Scholars', *Journal of Pentecostal Theology* 20 (2011), 213-31 (217-18). Levison's *Filled with the Spirit* (Grand Rapids: Eerdmans, 2009) was the topic of roundtable discussions in both *Journal of Pentecostal Theology* (issue 20.2) and *Pneuma* (issue 33.1).

son's insights, 'Spirit filling in the Old Testament is not a subsequent endowment but rather the *expansion* of the Spirit of life given to all humans from the time of Adam (Gen. 2.7) and even present in some sense in all flesh or creaturely life (Gen. 6.17)'.[43]

Now, of course, this kind of expansionist and broad approach to pneumatology has a way of creating a number of anxieties for many. The fears surrounding Levison's proposals not only relate to a particularization of the conventional understandings of subsequence that Pentecostals have used to solidify their presentation of Spirit baptism but also to what could amount to a reductive pneumatology generally. Macchia offers the following sobering words while using the first-person plural to speak of himself and other Pentecostals:

> As revivalists, we bathe in the glow of born-again Christianity and accent even more than other evangelicals the supernatural character of the Spirit's presence as a gift given to those who embrace Christ by faith. This accent on the supernatural and eschatological nature of the filling of the Spirit is not problematic in itself, except that we tend to think that we can only highlight this by neglecting the Spirit that inspires human wisdom and virtue 'from below', so to speak. We thus tend to see life outside of (or prior to) Christ as dark, lost, and devoid of the Holy Spirit. Our talk of spiritual gifts tends to highlight the extraordinary powers of the age to come that overtake us suddenly from above rather than the propensities granted from birth that the Spirit causes to flourish in our ongoing dedication to God's will. We tend to regard any celebration of the Spirit of life outside the sacred walls of the church as 'liberal' and denigrating of Christ's uniqueness.[44]

Macchia recognizes that Levison is simply trying to account for the complexity of Spirit-speech within the biblical canon itself and how it spans Israelite, Jewish, and Christian orbits. And part of this range opens the possibility for other pneumatological proposals, including ones inherent to the Jewish Scriptures; of the many pos-

---

[43] Frank D. Macchia, 'The Spirit of Life and the Spirit of Immortality: An Appreciative Review of Levison's *Filled with the Spirit*', *Pneuma* 33 (2011), pp. 70-71 (emphasis in original).

[44] Macchia, 'The Spirit of Life and the Spirit of Immortality', pp. 71-72.

sibilities from this multi-constituted testimony, one would be that 'the presence of the spirit of God is evident among those who cultivate virtue'.[45]

The moral-theological implications of such proposals are exceedingly vast, both in the way the Pentecostal subtradition negotiates its internal life as well as its outward impetus to the wider world. On the one hand, against longstanding suspicions, one can argue that an approach that moves 'from below to above' need not be a pneumatologically (and so theologically) devoid approach to moral formation. Quite the contrary, such an orientation would invite the dogmatic possibilities of interrelating the loci of pneumatology and creation so that they could deepen, strengthen, and sustain the Pentecostal revivalist impulses that, with the onset of time, have proven to be precarious without intentional attention and cultivation.

For instance, it is a lamentable feature of classical Pentecostalism's history that race relations became a stumbling block so early on in the movement's life. For all the promise that existed with such developments as William J. Seymour's leadership at the Azusa Street Revival as well as the ordination of white ministers by C.H. Mason and the Church of God in Christ, the conditions were ripe for classical Pentecostalism within America to provide an embodied sign of racial reconciliation and healing that would anticipate the soon-coming manifold reign of God's kingdom.[46] As students of the movement's history know, however, the opposite happened in that Pentecostalism capitulated to the segregationist pressures of the pre-Civil Rights era. Was this capitulation a failure of the Spirit's

---

[45] Levison, '*Filled with the Spirit*: A Conversation with Pentecostal and Charismatic Scholars', p. 217.

[46] Admittedly, some 'practical' needs were at play within some of these arrangements, such as the need of white ministers to have official ministerial credentials so that they could perform marriages and receive reduced railroad rates; nevertheless, one also finds cases like G.B. Cashwell, who testified that after a time of struggle regarding the African-American leadership of the Azusa revival he went on to 'suffer a crucifixion' so as to 'die to many things'; eventually, he requested Seymour and other blacks to pray for him, an act that was quickly followed by his experience of Pentecostal Spirit baptism (see H. Vinson Synan, 'Cashwell, Gaston Barnabas' in Stanley M. Burgess (ed.), *The New International Dictionary of Pentecostal and Charismatic Movements* [Grand Rapids: Zondervan, rev. and expanded edn, 2003], pp. 457-58 [hereafter cited as *DPCM*], and also *idem*, *The Holiness-Pentecostal Tradition: Charismatic Movements in the Twentieth Century* [Grand Rapids: Eerdmans, 1997], chapter 6).

work of adequately infusing the gift and grace of divine charity on the hearts of early Pentecostals? Or was the development more accurately a failure by these early adherents to translate and carry over the insights and impulses they experienced in the doxological modalities of abiding and waiting into quotidian living where habits, dispositions, desires, and 'second nature' or default behaviors are at play?

Obviously, the latter seems to be the case because a pattern of sorts manifested itself among early American Pentecostals: Many of the promising and countercultural – that is, gospel-indicating – features of Pentecostal life fell by the wayside over time. Racial, gender, generational, and doctrinal possibilities gave way to petty and hurtful divisions, ones which continue to plague the movement in its American instantiations. The pattern is of 'worldly' thinking and feeling creeping into what *Veritatis splendor* calls 'innerworldly' matters.[47] Particularly, when competing accounts of what it means to be human and what it means to flourish and be happy presented themselves to early Pentecostals, the tendency by many was to bifurcate 'sacred' and 'ordinary' space so that the encounters at the heart of Pentecostal worship, ones that were meant to transform and infuse the whole of the epicletic community, became stifled and reduced to privatistic religiosity. The failure appears to be one related to a reluctance of habituating the quasi-practices of abiding and waiting in such a fashion that they could perdure in the midst of moral and political pressures to do otherwise. Therefore, these considerations point to the need of the epicletic community to negotiate internally the Spirit's promptings so as to cultivate Christian virtue over and against worldly encroachments.

This affirmation of the Spirit working 'from below' would also have important implications for the way Pentecostals engage the wider world. The Spirit's presence and work are not limited to the Christian church, much less to the Pentecostal subtradition, and Levison hints at this possibility when he remarks, 'Although a pneumatology in which "the Spirit that inspired human wisdom and virtue 'from below'" may not lead directly to a thoroughgoing universalism, it does root in Scripture the possibility that people outside the borders of Christianity are able to cultivate virtue because

---

[47] *Veritatis splendor*, 36.

they attend to God's spirit within them'.[48] This point could go in any number of directions, including a topic that has garnered significant attention by Pentecostals recently, namely interreligious dialogue.[49] But another direction more pertinent to this study would be a workable Pentecostal account of the transcendentals such as truth, goodness, and beauty. Undoubtedly, Pentecostals would negotiate these classical values in a pneumatological framing, one constituted and inflected both by the witness of Scripture and the testimony emitting from those who have participated in Pentecostal worship, but given that these transcendental predicates of being[50] are appreciated by Pentecostals within their modality of worship and yet they are not limited to that context, an ongoing negotiation of how these can be instantiated within the 'economy of creation' is important for purposes of informing a Pentecostal account of theological anthropology as well as working proposals related to the implications of pre- and post-fall existence, ones that do not simply default to other, more developed evangelical options (particularly Wesleyan and Reformed alternatives).

One way of phrasing the matter is that creation's 'first perfection' requires attending to in order that it may cohere theologically with its 'second perfection'; of course, other dyads (nature/grace, natural law/evangelical law, and so forth) present themselves. But whatever the coupling of choice, the pneumatological implications are significant, as Levison and his interlocutors have pointed out; the same can be said for what is implied in Jürgen Moltmann's *The Spirit of Life*, a text also considered significantly by Pentecostals in the past.[51] The point to emphasize is that if the triune God is the source and end of truth, beauty, and goodness, and if Pentecostals believe these are instantiated and apprehended by the presence and work of the Holy Spirit, then an ongoing framework for adjudication is needed so that Pentecostals can see the Spirit's work when goodness is sought, truth is clarified, or beauty is displayed. To cite Thomas once again, 'All things desire God as their end, when they

---

[48] John R. Levison, 'Recommendations for the Future of Pneumatology', *Pneuma* 33 (2011), pp. 82-83.

[49] One thinks here of the many works by Amos Yong and Tony Richie.

[50] For a helpful exploration of such a category, see D. Stephen Long, *The Goodness of God: Theology, the Church, and Social Order* (Grand Rapids: Brazos, 2001), pp. 19-28.

[51] See *Journal of Pentecostal Theology* 4 (1994).

desire some good thing, whether this desire be intellectual or sensible, or natural, i.e. without knowledge; because nothing is good and desirable except forasmuch as it participates in the likeness to God'.[52] Given their imaginative capacities to welcome wonder and surprise, surely Pentecostals could come to see the search for goodness (as habituated in the cultivation of the virtues) as related to an account of pneumatological giftedness and actualization since humans are created in the *imago Dei* and destined for beatitude. If such is the case, then the pursuit of goodness, truth, and beauty would not be a-pneumatic activities, for doing so would cheapen the extent of the Spirit's work upon all flesh and all creation. The vision of the Spirit breathed upon and poured out on all flesh would effectually portray the entire world as the theatre of God's self-presentation, as an altar where God is moving and beckoning the creation in surprising and wondrous ways. This kind of pneumatic prevenience would be precisely the kind of worldview Pentecostals would find appealing, for it would heighten both the imagination and the sense of possibility since Godly, and not simply human, endeavoring would take center-stage.

5. Conclusion

The value of the Thomistic account of the virtues is that it moves from considerations related to what it means to be human and what it means to be blessed in one fell (albeit exceedingly nuanced and complicated) swoop. It is the kind of vision that can best sustain a Pentecostal self-understanding as a 'worldview' or as a way of 'being-in-the-world' because it is one that emits from the context of *sacra doctrina*, yet its reach is meant to extend to all that is. Without turning away from or cheapening the altar encounter, such a vision can portray God's work in the world as a coherent, multivalent, continuous whole: What God intended and did at creation has been progressing and moving along despite the rebellion and disobedience of God's creatures. What came or went out from God is returning to God in a manifold and glorious way. What is imperfectly seen or attended to now will be perduring and perfect when all of creation (including human selves) will be fully constituted and or-

---

[52] *ST*, I. q.44, a.4, r.3.

dered by the shalom and splendor of God's glory. If Pentecostals hold that the inbreaking kingdom of God is apprehended within the modality of Pentecostal worship, then 'abiding' and 'waiting' cannot simply be instances at the altar; they have to be habituated practice-orientations that foster a kind of 'second nature', a set of dispositions in relation to all that is. If Pentecostalism is to be portrayed as a way of 'being-in-the-world', then simply nothing less will do.

4

PURSUING HOLINESS IMPROVISATIONALLY

For a number of reasons, both historical and theological, Pentecostalism has been associated with the question of holiness. Many historians have made the point that Pentecostalism emerged from Holiness forebears, those who had drawn from the wells of the revivalist activities associated with the nineteenth century Holiness Movement. Theologically, the point was made time and time again that a dynamic was at play within Pentecostal circles of both purity and power. This dynamic was especially the case within the explicit branch of Wesleyan Pentecostalism, one that incorporated into its vision of the spiritual life the motifs of both sanctification/perfection and Spirit baptism. Significant diversity existed among early Pentecostals in interrelating purity and power within the rubrics of sanctification and Spirit baptism, and much of this variability had to do with the immediate religious background of Pentecostal adherents. As Vinson Synan put it, 'Since most of the early Pentecostal leaders had been prominent or active in the holiness movement, it seemed natural for them to maintain the place of sanctification as a "second blessing" that cleansed the seeker from "inbred sin", thus preparing for the reception of the Holy Spirit'.[1] But the logic came under duress as new adherents joined the movement: 'The problem over the second work', mentions Synan, 'arose when large numbers of converts began to enter the movement from non-Wesleyan backgrounds, notably the Baptist Churches. Not schooled in holiness theology, these people thought

---

[1] Synan, *The Holiness-Pentecostal Tradition*, p. 149.

of Christian experience as involving only two steps – conversion and the baptism with the Holy Ghost'.[2]

The spearhead of this later development was William Durham of Chicago, and his doctrine became known as the 'finished work' understanding, one that assumed that the salvific achievement of Calvary made the believer free from sin at the point of conversion; therefore, according to this logic, no need existed for a second work of grace. Essentially, without sensing the need to integrate the older Holiness paradigm with the emerging Pentecostal one, Durham collapsed justification and a particular understanding of sanctification into the work of salvation. Sanctification in turn became the divisive point that distinguished the 'four-' or 'five-fold gospel' paradigms, and given that the former was more generalizable as Pentecostalism grew into its own (that is, became increasingly distinguishable from its Holiness embers over time), the 'finished work' eventually became widespread,[3] thereby weakening the status of sanctification within Pentecostalism over time.

The collapse represented by Durham's theology led to a greater burden by Wesleyan Pentecostals to make their 'three-crises' paradigm 'do work' for their adherents. The matter was easy enough to account for when people continued to claim the distinct experience of sanctification; it became all the more tedious and difficult to preserve when the revivalist practices and confessions surrounding sanctification waned. At such junctures, older generations were at pains to bequeath a viable and coherent understanding of Christian religious experience to newer generations, and given the emergence and sensationalist flair of the Pentecostal ethos and its psychomotor displays, these newer generations privileged pentecostal power over sanctified purity. Sanctification became a middle step between salvation and Spirit baptism that many did not necessarily experience in the precise order that others did through the natural progression of moving from the Holiness fold to the emerging Pentecostal

---

[2] Synan, *The Holiness-Pentecostal Tradition*, p. 149.

[3] As Synan notes, the early Pentecostal denominations that had historical links to the Holiness Movement (for instance, the Church of God, the Pentecostal Holiness Church, and the Church of God in Christ) continued to advocate the second work of sanctification; nevertheless, the Pentecostal denominations that emerged from 1911 onward (including the Assemblies of God) were more inclined to the 'finished work' understanding (see Synan, *The Holiness-Pentecostal Tradition*, pp. 151-52).

Movement over the span of years early in the twentieth century. In all these matters, the precise nature of sanctification was in dispute, but such difficulty has always been inherent to those who would make holiness a vital feature of the Christian faith journey.[4]

1. Sanctification in Wesleyan Key across the Anglophone World

Sanctification in the nineteenth century American context experienced a significant shift away from its Wesleyan iteration in the eighteenth century, and this development no doubt was due in part to the tension-laden ambiguity of its originating circumstances. John Wesley was at great pains throughout his life to explain what he meant by the doctrine of entire sanctification/Christian perfection, and the matter was only complicated by his apparent shifts in opinion as he matured as preacher and theologian. In typical fashion, Wesley attempted a 'middle way' in recognizing both instantaneity and marked progression in the Christian life. He wanted to recognize the indisputability of a 'real change' in the heart of a believer while also taking into account the struggle in the present life to work against the 'inbred sin' that persists among the faithful. With his workable definition of entire sanctification or Christian perfection as involving 'perfect love of God and neighbor', Wesley did not want to shortchange the possibilities available to the Christian this side of Christ's resurrection and Pentecost. Entire sanctification, as distinguished from the initial sanctification or regeneration that occurs at the same time one is justified, was considered by Wesley in dispositional terms, that is, the approach of the Christian to God and everything else that is. Critics of Wesley, both in his lifetime and ever since, have wondered if his view involved an eradicationist impulse, which is to say that Christians in this life can be freed entirely and completely from the implications of sin. Given that Wesley consistently maintained that both growth and tempta-

---

[4] The Holiness Movement and its denominational progeny have endured this problem to such a degree that some have made the alarmist (and somewhat sensationalist) claim that the movement is 'dead'. See Kenneth Collins, 'Why the Holiness Movement is Dead', *Asbury Theological Journal* 54 (1999), pp. 27-35. At the heart of Collins's concerns, ones raised by Keith Drury earlier, is the inability of Holiness folks to transmit a viable understanding of entire sanctification/Christian perfection in the midst of waning revivalist fervor.

tion are always possible in the present life, the eradicationist suspicion is significantly moot despite its persistence by certain skeptics
and their appeal to certain quotes from Wesley.

Nevertheless, as the Holiness Movement emerged in the nineteenth century at different locales within the American scene, Wesley's nuances, as difficult as they were for him to maintain and
communicate, became even more of a challenge for his spiritual
progeny. Given revivalist pressures in addition to the American
penchant toward pragmatism (among other factors), sanctification
came to be largely understood as a singular instance, a revivalist experience along with salvation. Inevitably, a particular reception of
Wesley played a role here by those making a case that the transition
was actually the originating Wesleyan intent. For instance, the
wording of one of Wesley's most popular sermons indicates how
this reading could take place:

> 'But does God work this great work [of sanctification] in the
> soul *gradually* or *instantaneously?*' Perhaps it may be gradually
> wrought in some ... But it is infinitely desirable, were it the will
> of God, that it should be done instantaneously; that the Lord
> should destroy sin 'by the breath of his mouth' in a moment, in
> the twinkling of an eye.[5]

Wesley continues, 'If you seek [sanctification] by faith, you may expect it *as you are*: and if as you are, then expect it *now*'.[6] Passages like
these were used by certain Wesleyans and Methodists to portray
entire sanctification as instantaneous and available through the altar
encounter.

Although she was not alone in making this move, the approach
leaning toward instantaneity with regard to entire sanctification or
Christian perfection reached a pronounced representation in the
work of Phoebe Palmer. Palmer thought that she was a faithful fol-
lower of Wesley, but she did modify Wesley's theology in some important aspects.[7] Her 'shorter way' to holiness became synonymous

---

[5] 'The Scripture Way of Salvation', II, p. 168 (emphasis in the original).

[6] 'The Scripture Way of Salvation', II, p. 169 (emphasis in the original).

[7] Charles Edward White, documents these changes in *The Beauty of Holiness: Phoebe Palmer as Theologian, Revivalist, Feminist, and Humanitarian* (Eugene: Wipf and Stock, 2008), pp. 125-43. These alterations include the privileging of the instantaneous over the gradual, the conflation of sanctification language with Pentecostal imagery (including Spirit baptism) and the location of sanctification at the begin-

with an approach to sanctification that involved perfect consecration, faith, and testimony in what could easily devolve into a mechanistic and overly logical process. As with salvation, so with sanctification within this paradigm: The seeker had simply to believe and the matter would progress. God's will and purposes were all inclined to make sanctification a promised reality available to all who would have it; the variable, therefore, was simply whether a person would accept it. If the experience did not occur, the problem rested with the seeker: She simply was not trying hard enough and so not consecrating herself fully to the degree that she could. If she did manage to experience such a blessing, she was obligated to share it with others.

This nineteenth century understanding of sanctification perdured among the early ranks of Wesleyan Pentecostals so that the Pentecostal experience of Spirit baptism became one additional crisis experience that followed two previous ones (salvation and sanctification), but as noted above, the structure itself worked as long as people were claiming these experiences and had a tacit understanding of what was implied by each of them. Over time among this fluctuating group, the goal of the Christian life became the Pentecostal experience, making sanctification a gateway or meddlesome middle experience in the path to the fullness to come. Such understandings, sensibilities, and their ensuing practices only complicated the reception and function of sanctification within Pentecostal life. Soon, sanctification became an experiential cipher that increasingly meant little or caused what seemed to be unnecessary confusion for subsequent generations of Pentecostals.

In light of the vacuity of these developments, sanctification became associated largely with prohibitions and 'holiness codes' so as to provide the criteria necessary for distinguishing the sanctified believer from the profane sinner or even half-hearted believer. Any number of practices were considered forbidden by many within these fellowships; possibilities included gum-chewing, consuming caffeine, smoking, mixed bathing (swimming), movie-going, dancing, and others. An emphasis upon the strict observance of these prohibitions ensued so that over time they became ends unto themselves. A rampant legalism emerged so that one's style of dress or

---

ning of the Christian life rather than its end. What follows depends significantly on White's elaboration of Palmer's 'shorter way'.

one's outward appearance became the instantiating warrants for negotiating whether one was living a holy life that was pleasing to the Lord. Only through such adjudications could one know if one was honoring the biblical mandate to treat the body as the temple of the Holy Spirit. Naturally, as ends unto themselves, these prohibitions became excessively emphasized, and they all too often presented possibilities in which the exercise of Christian charity could be overshadowed by discriminating and judgmental attitudes.

Nevertheless, amidst the many difficulties surrounding these excessive emphases upon appearance and behavior, a kernel of truth was potentially on display by these would-be saints, and this sensibility was that participating in the kingdom of God involved not only an inward reconfiguration but an outward one as well. For all the disagreements one could have regarding what constitutes biblical 'modesty', at least these believers were attempting to reorder their lives in light of an account of what such a notion could mean within quotidian living. In other words, these Pentecostal believers had the sanctified impulse to follow the biblical mandates in pursuit of the holy life, and the fact that they made modifications within their own practices and lifestyles in light of such concerns demonstrates some awareness and openness that, when distinguished from the legalistic extremes, could prove helpful for the working out of one's salvation.

Over time, however, since prohibitions came to be emphasized more so than their theological rationales, a strong reaction against them ensued by subsequent generations. Any number of reasons for such reactions could be offered. For instance, the denial of an apparent taboo can become all the more attractive and desirable over time, making a capitulation to participate in it increasingly likely, especially when people 'come of age' or are not compelled by or brought to the understanding of the original warrants that led to its original formulation as a taboo. Second, many of these 'sanctified prohibitions' had to do with luxuries and excesses that many Pentecostals could not afford anyway, and so their resistance of identifying with worldly living may have had roots in a class-protest of sorts. However, with the 'redemption and lift' effect that so many Pentecostals eventually experienced, affordability became a decisive feature in negotiating what things continued to be taboos and what matters became simply indications of the bounty of God's favor.

Because theological rationales had often already been neglected by the time the questioning and resistance to these taboos took place, the theological warrants were not available and so were usually lost in the fray. In the overreaction to legalist approaches to modesty (to take but one example), both the legalist prohibitions and the biblical call to modesty were discarded in one fell swoop. These developments made sanctification as a topic all the more problematic for Wesleyan Pentecostals since it was often assumed to require such legalistic accoutrements. As Land notes of his own denomination, the transitions have been detrimental from the ethical point of view:

> The Church of God, Cleveland, Tennessee, for example, no longer has bans on jewelry, movies, etc. Now that more is affordable, it seems that more has become permissible ... As the story changed so did the ethic. *But no new unifying story has emerged to guide ethical behavior*, and 'affordability' is clearly neither a biblical nor a particularly theological satisfying ethical stance.[8]

The vacuum occasions a natural default to the status quo, which in the American context would mean at least the adoption of a consumerist logic for elaborating all that is holy and good.

What follows is a working proposal to account for the lacuna that Land points out. This alternative recognizes that the legalism of the past is not an option but neither is a contemporary antinomianism. Rather than operating at the deontological level of prohibitions and commandments, this proposal hopes to retrieve and sustain a logic that is more teleologically inclined, one that pivots on the epicletic understanding of Pentecostal fellowship that this study has highlighted thus far through its emphases on the poles of abiding and waiting. In particular, what follows is an approach to ecclesial holiness that is grounded in a robust account of the Spirit at work in believers so that they 'perform the faith' in a fashion that is both faithful but also attentive to the dynamics of being-in-the-world as a Spirit-imbued and Spirit-led fellowship. The approach involves the cultivation of the imagination in light of a familiarity with the parameters and possibilities of holy living; the dynamic is such that it suggests the life of the epicletic community to be im-

---

[8] Land, *Pentecostal Spirituality*, p. 66 n. 1 (emphasis added).

provisationally enacted over time in faithfulness to the call of Christ to follow, imitate, and abide in him.

2. The Pentecostal Penchant to Embody and Improvise

Pentecostals have always been naturally inclined to be 'doers', that is to say, they have made the connection between hearing/believing and embodying the faith quite naturally and intuitively. As a case in point, it has been argued that Pentecostals historically were quite pragmatic and innovative in the way they went about professing their message. Such innovation included the appropriation of strategies that included the use of the latest publishing technologies and transportation mediums available so that relatively shortly after revivals – whether these occurred in the Unicoi Mountains of Eastern Tennessee/Western North Carolina; Topeka, Kansas; or Los Angeles, California – Pentecostals were up and about witnessing of their deep and life-changing experiences of the triune God. The evangelistic and missionary zeal of the early Pentecostals must have been a sight to behold, for it is difficult to imagine how quickly and readily folks moved from a particular revivalist setting to the outer reaches of the world in what seemed to be one continuous movement.

As repeatedly noted in this study, the Pentecostal tendency to self-identify as a 'movement' rather than a 'church' and to think often of their activity as over and against ecclesial bodies makes for a challenging task when reflecting theologically about Pentecostalism. As such, the prominence of 'movement' language led to a certain improvisational quality about Pentecostal identity and practice. Given their self-understood place within unfolding history, early Pentecostals demonstrated a certain freedom in starting 'anew' in relation to ecclesial minutia.[9] For instance, the language of 'ordinances' has historically been more predominant than 'sacraments' among Pentecostals, and the understanding of sacramentality

---

[9] My quotes here attempt to show that the proclivity by Pentecostals to think of themselves as occupying a vital role in the denouement of history is inherently a modern sensibility. As R.G. Robins, *A.J. Tomlinson: Plainfolk Modernist* (Oxford: Oxford University Press, 2004), p. 24, has stated with regard to the Holiness precursors of the Pentecostal Movement, 'Those who flocked to holiness churches, tents, and camp meetings were drawn to the movement not because it resisted some overarching process of "modernization" but because it spoke to their modern needs and aspirations in a language with which they were familiar'.

(although not explicitly stated as such) has been understood to include both the worshipers' bodies and other quasi-sacramental rites.[10] Furthermore, baptismal services were sometimes impromptu wherever a body of water was available (in rivers, lakes, pools, and even bathtubs). In all this activity, there was a sense of 'making it up' as one went, especially with regard to ecclesial practices, and such activity brought with it a certain level of energy and expectancy.

Inevitably, when traditional formulations, practices, and understandings are suspended or reconfigured, great potential exists for both peril and promise. That which has been 'passed' down often is purposefully so, having been shaped and tried through different agonistic and tension-laden contexts. As many are prone to say, orthodoxy emerges within the precarious and contested context of formulating and discerning what is faithful from what is heretical. Lamentably, these tried and contested accomplishments were often neglected by Pentecostals when they understood themselves as over and against ecclesial institutions. Such posturing not only saw them fail to offer the peace of Christ to fellow sisters and brothers but in turn miss the continuity of the Spirit's work in the world over time. An unfair disparagement of others and an aggrandized view of themselves were sometimes the results.[11] In this regard, Pentecostals failed to be a holy fellowship, and their actions and motives are worth scrutinizing by contemporary Pentecostals in a probing, transparent, and contrite way as a means of healing ecumenical tensions.

And yet, tradition can also be reifying and stifling, and the advantage Pentecostals had in beginning 'anew' ecclesially was the vision and implementation of what seemed to them to be marks of God's kingdom. Rather than being led by 'man-made creeds' and customs, early Pentecostals enacted certain practices that were grounded in God's word and prompted by God's Spirit in such a way that they imagined a 'new order' for reality. Within this new order, it was understood that the lame could walk, the blind could

---

[10] See Amos Yong, 'Ordinances and Sacraments' in Stanley Burgess (ed.), *Encyclopedia of Pentecostal and Charismatic Christianity* (New York: Routledge, 2006), pp. 345-48.

[11] As a case in point, Peter Hocken notes that early in the movement's history certain groups believed that only those who had experienced Spirit baptism were members of the church; see Hocken, 'Church, Theology of the' in *DPCM*, p. 544.

see, and daughters could prophesy. In a hermeneutical move that had vast theological ramifications, Pentecostals have traditionally believed that the God who was at work in revealing Godself on Mount Sinai and on Calvary is the same God who is working in the context of Pentecostal worship. In this regard, Pentecostals have demonstrated themselves to be a holy fellowship when they have embodied and put in motion the implications of encountering this holy God.

The Pentecostal penchant for 'doing' suggests that holiness is not simply an attribute of God that solely marks the ineffable and unique Creator of all that is. Quite the contrary, Pentecostals have been inclined, given their robust approach to Scripture and the prominence of Jesus' life and ministry for their vision of reality, to think in terms of embodying and performing holiness. Such activities, of course, stand in tension with many Christian traditions and approaches that would think of holiness as the true, inimitable essence of God, that feature of God's existence that makes God who God is; when pushed, this logic would find problematic or at least worrisome the claim that humans participate or demonstrate holiness since agency in such a schema would shift the focus from the theological to the anthropological realm.[12]

Scripture, however, supports a multi-tiered approach to holiness. On a plain-sense reading, instances occur within the holy canon where holiness is attributed to those who engage in various practices associated with covenant-keeping.[13] Usually stemming from non-

---

[12] One sees this cautiousness in John Webster, *Holiness* (Grand Rapids: Eerdmans, 2003), especially chapter 3. Webster depends significantly on the Epistle to the Ephesians, the notion of election, and the wisdom of considering the church's sanctity as an 'alien sanctity' (56) for his work on holiness. He is explicitly aware of and attempting to avoid extremes, but his perspective does lean in a significant direction: 'The Church is holy; but it is holy, not by virtue of some ontological participation in the divine holiness, but by virtue of its calling by God, its reception of the divine benefits, and its obedience of faith. Like its unity, its catholicity and its apostolicity, the Church's holiness is that which it is by virtue of its sheer contingency upon the mercy of God' (p. 57). Since this publication, Webster has gone on to speak in more complementary ways regarding the interplay of divine and human action. For a treatment of his early reflections in *Holiness*, see Daniel Castelo, 'Holiness *Simpliciter*: A Wesleyan Engagement and Proposal in Light of John Webster's Trinitarian Dogmatics of Holiness', *Wesleyan Theological Journal* 47 (2012), forthcoming.

[13] Three examples from the Catholic Epistles offer a specific view on the matter: Jas 4.8 ('Cleanse [your] hands, sinners, and purify [your] hearts, double-minded ones'), 1 Pet. 1.22 ('You have purified your souls by obedience to the

Pauline sources, the collective testimony of this witness suggests that holiness is not simply something that characterizes believers on the basis of the effects of God's work in Christ but also a moral category that reaches into all of one's life as an implication of being transformed in, through, and by Christ. The tendency by many Pentecostals to think of their faith in terms of a spirituality further underscores the Pentecostal penchant to think of holiness not as something simply to be recognized of God's very self but a possibility to be enacted in the common life of the worshiping community.

Of course, what it means to purify a people's hearts, souls, or very selves is an open question in part because that which contaminates the epicletic community by its living in the world is so sinister. Because the filth of the world makes this fellowship impure in so many ways, embodying holiness must also take shape in multitudinous ways. Reifying the practice of holiness only has the potential for leading to a pharisaical works-righteousness; there has to be a certain communal liberty and dynamism involved in discerning what does and does not conform to God's purposes, both in the community's praxis and its collective affectional life. This discernment process is largely a form of epicletic abiding and waiting in that a community has to have its imagination illuminated to recognize both what is profane and how a sanctified approach to such profanity could look like. Additionally, whereas purifying oneself implies the 'negative' connotation of 'giving up' certain practices and habits, it also implies the 'positive' corollary of 'picking up' other habits and practices; both features involve an ongoing negotiation, one that is participatory and steadfast in its faithful orientation. Therefore, both in discerning that which does not conform to God and in the practices of 'putting aside' and 'picking up', embodied holiness by the epicletic community demonstrates an improvisational quality, one that is both coherent and yet free.

---

truth'), and 1 Jn 3.3 ('And everyone who has this hope purifies oneself on the basis of [God] just as [God] is pure'). I was directed to these canonical instances through conversations with my colleague Robert W. Wall; he will lay out a formal treatment of 'practicing holiness' from the New Testament witness in Daniel Castelo (ed.), *Holiness as a Liberal Art* (Eugene: Pickwick, forthcoming); biblical citations in this chapter are my translations.

3. Pneumatological Improvisation of Holiness

In response to critiques leveled at modernist assumptions about knowledge, proposals have arisen within the theological academy for thinking anew about the most faithful ways of approaching the holy mysteries. One such strategy has been through a serious engagement with the arts. This move has been made in different domains, but its generative force has been felt repeatedly.

In biblical studies, one sees this gesture in N.T. Wright's *The New Testament and the People of God*; in this work, Wright illustrates the notion of biblical authority as something to be enacted and heeded in an analogous way to how a Shakespearean play would be performed by well-trained actors if they had to improvise on what a missing fifth act would look like. The process would involve both consistency to the patterns that have gone before but also innovation given that the play is unfinished and so requiring some sort of development and a certain sense of completion.[14] Theologically understood, the narrative of Scripture could be enacted as authoritative by how the church understands and lives out its vocation in light of its role within its present situation, one that could be said to be an analogous 'Act 5' within the plot-line of Scripture's unfolding meta-narrative. Although different from Wright in important ways, other scholars have pursued similar imagery to shape and cast biblical interpretation.[15]

In theological studies, Kevin J. Vanhoozer's *The Drama of Doctrine* offers its readers a sustained effort in extending this theatrical metaphor to the realm of theology through his proposal of a 'canonical-linguistic' model. In particular, Vanhoozer argues that Christian doctrine is dramatic in that at stake is 'following "the Way" as the people of God enter new and uncharted intellectual and cultural territory'.[16] He believes doctrine can serve a dramaturgical role as it mediates between textual knowledge and creative performance in a wisdom-inducing fashion; therefore, Scripture

---

[14] N.T. Wright, *The New Testament and the People of God* (Minneapolis: Fortress, 1992), pp. 140-41.

[15] These include Nicholas Lash, *Theology on the Way to Emmaus* (Eugene: Wipf and Stock, 2005), chapter 3 and Frances Young, *The Art of Performance: Towards a Theology of Holy Scripture* (London: Darton, Longman and Todd, 1990).

[16] Kevin J. Vanhoozer, *The Drama of Doctrine: A Canonical Linguistic Approach to Christian Theology* (Louisville: Westminster John Knox, 2005), p. 22.

provides the script for the holy life that has to be enacted in the company of other actors. In this sense, doctrine provides 'dramatic direction' and the Christian life is depicted as 'performance interpretation.'[17]

In the company of these scholars, Samuel Wells has become a leading voice in interrelating the metaphor of improvisation with Christian ethics, and so his work will be the chief focus in what follows. Much of what he says bears resonances with the authors surveyed above, but his focus on ethical reflection is especially generative for the shape of Christian discipleship. According to Wells, 'Improvisation in the theater is a practice through which actors seek to develop trust in themselves and one another in order that they may conduct unscripted dramas without fear'.[18] Wells sees this practice as analogous to the ethical task of the church, for he hopes to show 'how the church may become a community of trust in order that it may faithfully encounter the unknown of the future without fear'.[19] The value of thinking of Christian ethics broadly as improvisation is that it assumes both a ruled-account of tradition and yet a certain freedom in its performance; Wells continues: 'There is a dimension of Christian life that requires more than repetition, more even than interpretation – but not so much as origination, or creation de novo ... When improvisers are trained to work in the theater, they are schooled in a tradition so thoroughly that they learn to act from habit in ways appropriate to the circumstance'.[20] The task of being 'faithful improvisers', that is, faithful disciples of Christ, requires a way of life that both shapes its members so that they are thoroughly ingrained into the tradition and yet that shaping constitutes a certain *habitus* by which the future, with all its vicissitudes and uncertainties, can be faced with confidence and hope.

Three features of Wells' use and exploration of the notion of improvisation for Christian ethics stand out for the present task. First, faithful improvisation beckons an ecclesial framework rather than an individualist approach. Wells has in mind a cadre of performers/improvisers on the grand stage of redemptive history who

---

[17] Vanhoozer, *The Drama of Doctrine*, p. 30.

[18] Samuel Wells, *Improvisation: The Drama of Christian Ethics* (Grand Rapids: Brazos, 2004), p. 11.

[19] Wells, *Improvisation*, p. 11.

[20] Wells, *Improvisation*, p. 65.

learn from one another how to embody the practice of faithful discipleship; he cites Jeremy Begbie's reading of the book of Acts as 'a stream of new, unpredictable, improvisations'.[21] From this testimony one sees that the early church faced a number of new and unforeseen circumstances in which it had to demonstrate covenant-fidelity, yet there was no precedent for much of what these early believers were facing, making the task of discernment ever so crucial for their life together.

Second, improvisation grants a certain 'freedom within boundaries' that is necessary for the enactment and embodiment of holiness. If holiness is assumed to be the way the church embodies the reign of God in such a manner that it demonstrates to the world both what it means to be the world and what it means to be the church, then a conceptual alternative would be helpful, one that can accommodate the need of a Christian community to maintain borders/distinctives in an open-ended way. Improvisation, when considered an ecclesial practice that involves both habituation and skill,[22] can help overcome the way the institutional and charismatic dimensions of ecclesial life are thought to be antagonistic to one another by allowing for both objective (Paul) as well as subjective (Catholic Epistles) features of performance for the understanding and enactment of holiness.

Finally, improvisation in the Christian moral sense is inherently and necessarily pneumatological. Wells does mention this feature of ecclesial improvisation, but he could have developed the matter further: Ecclesial improvisation does not simply rest on the talents, habits, and gifts of improvisers, but in a more determinative way, this process occurs in the church by the shaping, discipline, promptings, and call of the Holy Spirit. This pneumatological casting makes faithful improvisation part and parcel to the field of moral theology, for it is intrinsically tied to the modality of worship,

---

[21] Wells, *Improvisation*, p. 66, citing Jeremy Begbie, *Theology, Music, and Time* (Cambridge: Cambridge University Press, 2000), pp. 222-23. As its title suggests, Begbie's approach to improvisation is through the lens of musicology whereas Wells opts for the context of the theatre. In this section from which the quote is drawn, Begbie has some very suggestive remarks about the way the Spirit improvises in our midst out of what Jesus has done by 'hooking into' our realities and anticipating the age which is to come.

[22] Wells, *Improvisation*, chapter 5 is very helpful in elaborating improvisation in terms of a virtue or skill that is fostered by the church's worship and performance over time.

one which Wells does emphasize: 'For Christians the principle practice by which the moral imagination is formed, the principal form
of discipleship training, is worship'.[23]

When Pentecostals were truly operating under the direction of
the Holy Spirit, something was at play akin to Wells' vision of theological and ecclesial improvisation. Pentecostals had a heightened
sense of the possibilities for the future, and these stemmed partially
from both their restorationist primitivism and their modified dispensational premillennialism. They desired the kingdom and believed that it was on display in their lives and worship services as
the Spirit gave witness. They believed this inbreaking kingdom to
be a holy order, one that recreated, reconfigured, and called for a
reimagining of social arrangements, ecclesial practices, and individual piety.

4. The Case of Footwashing

One potential demonstration of this kind of ecclesial improvisation
among Pentecostals was the enactment and to some degree sacra-
mentalizing of footwashing. The practice itself was not entirely an
improvisational expression since one can see the activity enacted by
Jesus in John 13; it was also a practice that had a history within the
broader Mediterranean world of the first few centuries, and because
of Jesus' example, it was occasionally picked up by Christians in
varying circumstances.[24] During medieval times the practice came
to be associated with Maundy Thursday, the day of Holy Week in
which the 'command' of Jesus for his disciples to love one another
(Jn 13.34) was recognized for all of its implications regarding servitude and humility. However, the rite of washing the saints' feet has
had a variegated history, and it has rarely been viewed as a sacramental act, although definitionally (for instance, as a 'visible sign of
an invisible grace') one could justify its conception as such; there-

---

[23] Wells, *Improvisation*, p. 82 (the theme of worship is further extended in pag-
es 82-85).

[24] For some background to the practice, see the summary piece by John
Christopher Thomas, 'Footwashing within the Context of the Lord's Supper', in
Dale R. Stoffer (ed.), *The Lord's Supper: Believers' Church Perspectives* (Scottdale: Herald Press, 1997), pp. 169-84, and his more extensive treatment in John Christopher Thomas, *Footwashing in John 13 and the Johannine Community* (JSNTS 61; Sheffield: JSOT Press, 1991).

fore, it is true that Pentecostals were not unique in their appropriation of the practice of footwashing.[25]

Nevertheless, that the practice of footwashing was even adopted by Pentecostals is suggestive of another dimension of the Pentecostal ecclesial ethos. Historically, Pentecostals have tended not to be very self-consciously sacramental. As noted above, many Pentecostals have traditionally felt more at ease to talk about 'ordinances' rather than 'sacraments', the former term suggesting to Pentecostals acts of faithfulness undertaken by the command of Jesus to remember and imagine the implications of Christ's work rather than (as the latter term often suggested to them) acts that by their execution are efficacious (*ex opere operato*). And yet, these believers managed to see this practice of footwashing in John 13 as one meriting obedience and imitation, a move that had important theological ramifications for demonstrating what in fact the Spirit was doing in their midst.[26] For all the anti- or non-sacramental stereotypes circulated about Pentecostals, Frank Macchia believes that they have traditionally and consistently found such rites as footwashing and the laying on of hands for healing as those encounters of God that manifest the 'greatest power'.[27] If this observation is true, then what

---

[25] For a survey of the different Pentecostal contexts in which footwashing was practiced among early adherents, see John Christopher Thomas, 'Footwashing', *White Wing Messenger* 78 (November 2000), pp. 10-13.

[26] I find peculiar that Harold Hunter denies this improvisational feature of Pentecostal fellowship on the basis of normative assertions: 'Some pentecostal groups have practiced footwashing as an ordinance. Such an insistence wrongly infers a moral necessity in Jesus' actions that should be applied only to water baptism and the Eucharist. This object lesson in humility, as portrayed by Christ, is not an extraneous rite' (Hunter, 'Ordinances, Pentecostal', *DPCM*, p. 948). The language of 'moral necessity' as well as 'object lesson' does not accurately reflect the role and function of footwashing among those Pentecostals who practiced it. When coming to the text 'anew', these Pentecostals saw matters differently. To use the language of Begbie, Pentecostals tended from time to time to particularize the 'cultural restraints' within broader Christian expressions in the face of the 'occasional restraints' that they enacted through their worship and reading practices. It is no surprise then that a Pentecostal scholar could observe, 'When compared with the words of institution associated with water baptism and the Lord's Supper in the New Testament, the commands to wash feet appear to be the most emphatic of the three' (Thomas, 'Footwashing Within the Context of the Lord's Supper', p. 174). New possibilities open up when dominant restraints are suspended for a time.

[27] Frank Macchia, 'Is Footwashing the Neglected Sacrament?', *Pneuma* 19 (1997), p. 242.

is the significance of the practice of footwashing for the Pentecostal way of life as it is imagined in terms of the epicletic community?

Given the logic of improvisational holiness sustained in this chapter, one could argue that the adoption of footwashing by some Pentecostals took shape initially as an ecclesial activity of a semi-improvisational kind, one that marked a holy kind of fellowship as indicated by the leveling and empowering work of the Holy Spirit surrounding such a rite. Pentecostal fellowship purifies itself and demonstrates the holy reign of God in such practices as footwashing where structures of privilege, power, and difference are called into question in doxologically impromptu ways before the Lamb who was slain, the one who displayed the nature and character of God through his acts of self-giving, renunciation, and solidarity. Pentecostals are not alone in appropriating footwashing as a quasi-sacramental rite, but what is remarkable about the Pentecostal context is that this practice was even appropriated by a fellowship that traditionally emphasizes power. That a movement like Pentecostalism can employ a practice like footwashing within a setting like Pentecostal worship suggests that Pentecostals had a keen sense from whom and in what setting they were empowered.[28] Given all the options and possibilities available for habituating their ecclesial life together, that certain Pentecostals felt led to 'pick up' and 'hook into' the gospel narrative in this particular way betrays a pneumatic prompting, one that was Spirit-led and Christ-shaped.

Pentecostals stumbled upon a practice that they had paltry few theological resources to narrate for its full implications within their common life; however, it is also true that the impression is often more powerful than the narration. Jean Vanier, the founder of L'Arche communities, seems to agree; as he notes:

> At special moments in L'Arche and in Faith and Light, we wash each other's feet as an expression of our love. It is always very moving for me when someone with disabilities washes my feet

---

[28] In performing Jesus' practices, Pentecostals were engaging in a form of *imitatio Christi* that John Howard Yoder believed was the only way such imitation could be pursued: 'There is thus but one realm in which the concept of imitation holds ... This is at the point of the concrete social meaning of the cross in its relation to enmity and power. Servanthood replaces dominion, forgiveness absorbs hostility. Thus – and only thus – are we bound by New Testament thought to "be like Jesus"' (John Howard Yoder, *The Politics of Jesus* [Grand Rapids: Eerdmans, 2nd edn, 1994], p. 131).

or when I see a person wash the feet of their mother or father. It is the world turned upside down. In 1998 the Central Committee of the World Council of Churches in Geneva asked me to animate a day on spirituality. I suggested that after my talk, all the members of this Central Committee, representing some 230 different Christian churches, be invited to wash each other's feet during a special liturgy. It was particularly moving to witness an Orthodox bishop kneeling down and washing the feet of an American woman who was a Baptist minister. Gestures sometimes speak louder and more lastingly than words. It was a moment of both grace and unity.[29]

And by virtue of being one in which the 'world was turned upside down' because of the example of Jesus and the leading of the Holy Spirit, this enactment of footwashing at such a time and place was an improvisational particularization of embodied and practiced holiness.[30]

The Pentecostal Movement 'turned the world upside down' because it typified a kind of fellowship in which the lot of humanity is considered hungry, poor, and needy before God, and in that acknowledgment of human deficiency and divine sufficiency, holy power was thought to be available to all who would heed the call to follow Jesus. This dialectic of purity and power, of *mortificatio et vivificatio*, is at the heart of what was at work when social convention was particularised and radical arrangements were proposed, be they in relation to different kinds of human categories of stratification (for example, race, gender, and age) or institutions (such as established churches and the state).

---

[29] Jean Vanier, *Drawn into the Mystery of Jesus through the Gospel of John* (New York: Paulist Press, 2004), p. 230.

[30] In elaborating the dynamics of tradition and freedom in light of musical improvisation, Begbie remarks, 'What of paintings, missionary activity, the testimonies of prisoners, Bible-study groups in remote churches? These improvisations are potentially as fruitful and liberating as anything issuing from a committee of priests, and they themselves will often prove their worth by repeated particularisation in radically different situations' (Begbie, *Theology, Music and Time*, p. 217; emphasis added).

5. Sanctified Improvisation as Emitting from the Divine Character

The imagination required for the improvisation of holiness rests on the form of Christ's life, and so to take the example above, the dialectic of purity and power is on display quite vividly in the Johannine depiction of Jesus washing the disciples' feet. One who attends to the context of Jesus' world would not be surprised of Mary anointing Jesus' feet in John 12. John 13, however, presents another matter altogether. Given the coarseness of the activity because of its association with one of the most exposed parts of the body, footwashing took place in a number of specific circumstances. Sometimes, family members engaged in the activity, which demonstrated a level of trust and intimacy. In other circumstances, the host would wash the feet of a guest in an act of hospitality. Most often, slaves would engage in this activity, although Jewish slaves were not required to participate in such a practice on behalf of their masters. All in all, the activity functioned in a dual way: either as a sign of grace and love or as an obligation that those lower on the social scale would have to perform. Both dynamics, footwashing as a sign of intimacy or social stratification, pivot on this act being one of cleansing; only select people under select circumstances and arrangements come into contact with one's filth.[31]

That Jesus chose to wash the disciples' feet during and not before the supper suggests that he was intentionally showing them something of significance,[32] and given Peter's reaction, the incident was quite unusual. From one perspective, Peter's initial refusal of Jesus' act of cleansing suggests that he had in mind the stratification that marks human relationships as a whole; after all, here is Peter's rabbi, his *kurios*, who is wishing to wash his feet.[33] Jesus' response is telling: 'If I do not wash you, you have no part with me' (Jn 13.8).

---

[31] Thomas remarks, 'Due to its humble nature, the performance of such an act demonstrates tremendous affection, servitude, or both' (Thomas, *Footwashing in John 13 and the Johannine Community*, p. 42).

[32] When taking into account the canonical witness, the incident may be related to the internal strife on display in Luke 22 regarding who among the disciples was the greatest.

[33] One should not ignore what a revolutionary act this was: According to Thomas, 'Jesus' action is unparalleled in ancient evidence, for no other person of superior status is described as voluntarily washing the feet of a subordinate' (Thomas, *Footwashing in John 13 and the Johannine Community*, p. 59).

Obviously, Jesus had something in mind other than propriety or social convention. Through this single act of holy improvisation, Jesus called into question both what intimacy and authority mean in the kingdom of God.

The epicletic community, the Pentecostal fellowship, is holy to the degree that it knows and experiences this Jesus as the Lord and Giver of life. A holy fellowship is one of ongoing abiding in the Holy One of Israel who 'went out into the far country' and dwelt among us and extended and opened his very self to us. If Jesus is the truest and most accessible demonstration of who God is and what God is like, then one could argue that in Christ we see the truest and most accessible expression of God's holiness.[34] We see in him the dynamic of *mortificatio et vivificatio*, both in his life and in the order that he proclaims and initiates.

This christological note suggests that God's character is on display in a radical way through Jesus' act of washing the disciples' feet. Jesus acknowledges that there is a vast difference between the disciples and him: 'You call me Teacher and Lord – and you speak rightly, for I am' (Jn 13.13). He claims his authority in this passage but does so in order to call it into question in a crucial way: Jesus' authority rests not on the exercise of power or might according to conventional human standards but through the enactment of servitude, humility, and yes, washing another person's filth. Rather than perpetuating the social, philosophical, and theological patterns of the day in which holiness, privilege, and all that is deemed sacrosanct must be preserved and so separate from that which is dirty, fleeting, and coarse, Jesus shows something altogether different. This act is not simply an 'object lesson'; it is a sign of God's holy, inbreaking reign into the world, one in which the kenotic quality of all that is involved with incarnation is on display in a scandalizing and 'turning-the-world-upside-down' kind of way.

---

[34] Jason Goroncy reminds us that to speak of the holy in a thoroughly Christian way is 'to speak of none other than One who has bared his holy arm in Jesus Christ and by the Holy Spirit as the "Holy One in our midst", as our Redeemer and Sanctifier. In other words, we must never think of God's holiness (or human holiness) in abstraction from the action of the Triune God who elects, judges, saves and sanctifies humanity in Jesus Christ' (Jason Goroncy, 'The Elusiveness, Loss and Cruciality of Recovered Holiness', *International Journal of Systematic Theology* 10 [2008], p. 201).

Pentecostals have intuitively sensed that power from God stems from what Jesus has promised and done, including his work as sanctifier. The repeated emphasis on anointing and power by Pentecostals rests on a 'full gospel' that hinges on the identity and work of Christ. Sadly, this understanding tends to quantify and commodify power as a 'something' individuals have. Such inclinations are brimming with a number of threatening dangers, including an unhealthy sense of independence and individuality that can allow the church to think of itself as powerful apart from God. It is here where the push by some to consider Pentecostalism as a spirituality is key: The source of power is not from human selves but from the triune God, and participating and abiding in this life, a possibility which Christ has offered, is the only way to partake of such power. In other words, the shape of this power matters: In the case of Jesus' example in John 13, the power is 'other-directed'. As Barth notes, 'How emphatically the [Fourth Gospel's portrayal of the footwashing] emphasises the fact that the service of Christ is His true power and majesty and therefore the grace by which man receives his life'.[35]

Abiding in or staying on the vine (John 15) implies a continual attentiveness, one in which the whole body need not be washed but certainly the feet as one peregrinates in a vile world (Jn 13.10). The implication of such imagery within the Johannine testimony for the broader call of discipleship is that 'remaining' in Jesus is both an embarrassingly intimate and personally and socially disarming reality, one that implies continual 'pruning/cleansing' (Jn 15.2-3) on God's part to sanctify us in the midst of a hostile world. It is in this dynamic of vulnerability and dependency that Christ can be wondrously apprehended and powerfully proclaimed as the one who makes holy, that is, the one who sanctifies.

6. The Ontological, Moral, and Ultimately Doxological Question

Pentecostals in the past have struggled mightily with how to define and sustain a holy fellowship. Because of the complexity of the is-

---

[35] Karl Barth, *Church Dogmatics*, III/4 (ed. G.W. Bromiley and T.F. Torrance; Edinburgh: T & T Clark, 1961), p. 476.

sues involved, sometimes it was easier to appeal to a standardized list in order to make the task more manageable and assuring. The point of Pentecostal fellowship, however, is not to codify its collective life but to 'encounter the life of this crucified and risen Christ in the power of the Spirit'.[36] Such an encounter entails following Christ in improvisational and yet faithful ways: 'If you know these things, blessed are you if you do them' (Jn 13.17). The performance of holiness is a Christ-enabled possibility and command (see Jn 13.14) that is required for the epicletic community to grow in grace. In this growth, this fellowship follows and attends to the Holy One of Israel, its master, the one who has sent it (see Jn 13.16), and ultimately the one who loves it 'until the end' (Jn 13.1).

The holiness that marks Pentecostal fellowship can never be reified or codified, for doing so would compromise a fruitful and innovative (that is, a Spirit-empowered and Spirit-led) future. When early Pentecostals practiced footwashing, advocated pacifism, recognized women as partners in ministry, and held services of diverse racial backgrounds, they did so not on the basis of maintaining a level of relevance by their observance of the status quo; quite the contrary, their apparent irrelevance to the conventions of their day was the bedrock of their alarming relevance, that feature that made them eccentric in a holy kind of way. They may not have understood what they were doing (see Jn 13.7), but contemporary observers are coming to understand more and more the way the Spirit was leading this fellowship in the ways of holiness.

These believers improvised in holy ways as they caught glimpses of God's kingdom and in turn attempted to live in conformity with what they 'saw'. When some encountered the practice of footwashing as depicted in John 13, they went on to incorporate it into their communal life. It would seem that the future for the holiness of Pentecostal fellowship rests on its ability to 'abide' in the presence of Christ through the Spirit in such a way as to see and enact this holy reign in scriptural and yet unscripted ways. This dynamic of 'scripturally-unscripted improvisation' could mean anointing somebody with oil or washing another's feet; providing aid to relief organizations at the time of a natural disaster or refusing to bear arms in a war-crazed nation-state; or reaching out to the pariahs and 'un-

---

[36] Macchia, 'Is Footwashing the Neglected Sacrament?', p. 243.

touchables' of a given society or seeking those who are spiritually lost in a specific neighborhood. Whenever and wherever Christians are prompted, quickened, and led by the Spirit to engage in the work of the kingdom in a scriptural, timely, and prophetic way, there is enacted a *holy* Christian fellowship.

To conclude, the holiness of Pentecostal fellowship is both a moral task and an ontological reality, and both features are subsumed and sustained within the agent-related indeterminacy implied by the modality of Pentecostal worship. Unfortunately, it is not a given that within a particular Pentecostal fellowship people will continually and in a sustained way 'encounter the life of this crucified and risen Christ in the power of the Spirit'. Abiding in the triune God is precarious precisely because it involves an ongoing recognition of both dependence on Another and the insufficiency of the self. However, such dispositions and sensibilities mark the epicletic community, the fellowship for which 'worship absorbs the world'.[37] In such a setting, holiness is a grace-enabled possibility that is subsequently a function of ongoing confession, praise, humble receptivity, and faithful performance.

---

[37] This phrasing is a Pentecostal variant of George Lindbeck's famous remark of the 'text absorbing the world' in Lindbeck, *The Nature of Doctrine*, p. 118.

5

REFRAMING ESCHATOLOGICAL EXPECTATION

Patience is not an attribute one usually associates with Pentecostals. They are sometimes said to reflect uncritically modernist culture and to be technologically innovative, pragmatic, passionate, and even loud.[1] Pejorative characterizations often include 'holy rollers' and 'fanatics'; sometimes they are called 'possessed', 'mentally unstable', 'delusional', and 'deprived'.[2] We are often known for our fervor, one that can be positively described as 'sanctified urgency' or negatively as 'reckless impulsiveness'. But of all these characterizations, patience is not one that readily comes to mind.

A way in which this 'sanctified urgency' potentially gave way to a 'reckless impulsiveness' was early Pentecostalism's approach to missionary work. Commenting on this feature of the Azusa Street meetings, that revival that many associate with spawning much of Pentecostalism's global reach, Cecil M. Robeck remarks:

> Essentially, when someone spoke in a tongue, the mission followed a simple four-step program. First, they attempted to identify the language. Second, if they felt they had identified it, they sought to establish whether the speaker believed he or she had received a missionary 'call'. Third, if the tongues-speaker claimed to have such a call, the mission staff tried to discern whether the

---

[1] Pentecostals show a certain flair and dependence on cultural modernism and pragmatism, despite their restorationist heritage, making R.G. Robins' depiction of A.J. Tomlinson as a 'plainfolk modernist' a helpful representation of the movement as a whole.

[2] The most famous diatribe, of course, is associated with G. Campbell Morgan and the characterization of Pentecostalism as 'the last vomit of Satan'.

call was genuine and whether the person was ready and willing to go. Finally, if the person testified to a readiness to go, and the mission discerned the necessary gifts and call, then they gave the candidate the money to reach the foreign field.[3]

Through this description, one can see that this discernment process was deliberate and prayerful, but due process may have given way to expediency in that the candidate often 'left town within days, if not hours' to carry out the call.[4] Missionary financial support sometimes exhibited 'one-way ticket' support to the country of destination in the sense that these missionaries received enough money to reach their destinations but not enough for them to return.[5] The theological reasoning for such provision was that the immediate return of the Lord negated the need for funds to return home. If by chance the eschaton should be delayed, then God would provide for the missionary's needs.

This practice reveals a theological rationale for a kind of self-understood 'sanctified impatience', and it was thoroughly framed as eschatological. William Faupel has argued that eschatology was the heartbeat or the hermeneutical key for understanding early Pentecostalism,[6] and in making such a claim, Faupel was following the lead of Anderson, who believed that eschatological framing served as a mythos for the early movement as a whole.[7] From this impetus, one can detect from time to time within the early literature an 'over-realized' or 'hyper-realized' eschatology in which the 'already' was emphasized to the neglect of the 'not yet' in that the theological explanation for the miracles and gifts on display in Pentecostal worship was that Jesus' return was on the horizon. For first generation

---

[3] Cecil M. Robeck, Jr, *The Azusa Street Mission and Revival: The Birth of the Global Pentecostal Movement* (Nashville: Thomas Nelson, 2006), p. 239.

[4] Robeck used the test case of the Garrs and their eventual missionary journey to India to illustrate this process; see Robeck, *The Azusa Street Mission and Revival*, p. 239.

[5] Robeck, *The Azusa Street Mission and Revival*, p. 240.

[6] Faupel, *The Everlasting Gospel*, p. 20.

[7] Anderson, *Vision of the Disinherited*, p. 89. Anderson later notes, 'The gift of tongues … was considered a sign of Baptism in the Spirit, but that Baptism was only one aspect of the "Latter Rain" outpouring of the Spirit which was itself a sign of the Second Coming. The early Pentecostals did not consider speaking in tongues the message of their movement, but rather a means by which the message was confirmed, legitimized and propagated. The message was "Jesus is coming soon"' (p. 90).

Pentecostals, they believed they were participating in the 'latter rain', in a 'time before the time' when Jesus would return.[8] The Spirit was readying the world for the second coming of Christ, and those who knew and experienced this spiritual reality were called to share their faith in preparation for the 'marriage supper of the Lamb'.[9] With such a plausibility and interpretive structure, these saints were able to endure and undertake a number of sacrificial endeavors, including uprooting families and traveling to foreign lands in order to preach the Pentecostal blessing. The theological and praxis-oriented impulse for the proclamation of the 'full gospel' was an expectation of God's inbreaking kingdom.

This eschatological understanding worked for the early adherents of the movement, but with the passing of decades, eschatological urgency inevitably dwindled among the Pentecostal fold. Reference is rarely made to Jesus' second coming in today's American Pentecostal instantiations, and such a transition inevitably occasions the need for this subtradition to rethink its theological identity. The matter has to be both a retrieval and re-envisioning of the whole. If the fulfillment of eschatological expectation served as the impetus for early Pentecostalism's 'sanctified urgency', what to do now that the movement has entered its second century of existence? If, as Faupel and others have argued, the hermeneutic for the movement's self-understanding was a kind of eschatological self-placement and localization (so that the Pentecostal Movement signals the impending age to come), does the delay of the parousia not require a significant reconfiguration of what the movement means within the economy of God's self-disclosure and activity? The challenge is stark and to some degree overwhelming. Whether they have liked it or not, Pentecostals have been made to wait for what many thought was simply on the brink. This 'forced patience' could be in the long-run a double-edged sword. On the one hand, Pentecostals may be forced to look at the early figures of the movement and en-

---

[8] Peter Althouse considers at length the metaphor of the 'latter rain' within Pentecostalism in Peter Althouse, *Spirit of the Last Days: Pentecostal Eschatology in Conversation with Jürgen Moltmann* (London: T & T Clark, 2003), chapter 1.

[9] Althouse remarks that such metaphors as the 'bride of Christ' served to explain to Pentecostals that what they were witnessing was a climax of history. Such historical accoutrements helped sustain a rationale for such signs in the present as well as the reason why they were believed to be largely absent in the post-apostolic period. See Althouse, *Spirit of the Last Days*, p. 19.

gage in the difficult, but ultimately salutary, task of evaluating what theological motifs and rationales can and cannot be reworked and used for the present situation. On the other hand, this 'forced patience' could occasion the worrisome if not devastating development of a kind of self-willed blindness, one that refuses to look to the past and simply 'takes matters as they come', thereby occasioning a distinct identity so that conformity and defaulting to a broadly Evangelical status quo take effect. To persist with the imagery of Cheryl Bridges Johns, American Pentecostals could potentially persist in an unresolved identity crisis and in turn lose much of who they are in the process.[10]

Unfortunately, in one sense, such adjustments have already taken place to some degree, and the consequences have been dire. As Anderson presciently noted, a shift in theological accents has taken place within Pentecostalism so that now Pentecostal self-understanding in terms of identity and mission largely revolves around the role of glossolalia and the experience of baptism in the Spirit more so than the end-times expectation of the kingdom (in which the manifestation of tongues plays a role).[11] Such a shift no doubt creates conditions in which the commodification and inordinate emphasizing of the experience of Spirit baptism (alongside its criterion for identification – tongues) take place, moves that, when sustained, may have the counter-effect of working against the perpetuation of the Pentecostal ethos. As noted repeatedly in this study, the pursuit of a spiritual experience is largely an individualized and privatized affair apart from an abiding and perduring fellowship to sustain, uplift, and chasten the seeker. When left to their own, individual seekers of privatized religious experience will simply find such experiences both initially exciting but also transformatively and theologically short-lived.

In light of these shifts, Pentecostal eschatological expectancy is in tatters within the American context. An editorial by Frank Macchia suggests as much when he ponders the role of eschatology within the movement more broadly; he asks the pressing question:

---

[10] Cheryl Bridges Johns, 'The Adolescence of Pentecostalism: In Search of a Legitimate Sectarian Identity', *Pneuma* 17 (1995), pp. 3-17.

[11] See Anderson, *Vision of the Disinherited*, pp. 96-97; this argument is largely assumed by Dayton, *Theological Roots of Pentecostalism* and Faupel, *The Everlasting Gospel*.

'Were the Pentecostals mistaken at the turn of the century when they shared the apostle's conviction [of Romans 13.11-12] in their time as well?'[12] The question raises broader issues related to Pentecostal identity and self-understanding: How do Pentecostals understand their history and their future in light of Christ's own eschatological tarrying? Christ has not returned despite expectations, so how can current Pentecostals deal with their heritage of 'impatience' in light of the Lord's own patience in delaying the parousia?

The task for Pentecostals at present is to recast their theological self-understanding and their sense of what eschatological expectation ought to look like. The contention of this concluding chapter on Pentecostal moral theology is that the eschatological expectation that marked early American Pentecostalism was not something that these saints had necessarily contrived in all of its features since *God's kingdom*, as they experienced it in Pentecostal worship, *was breaking into the world*; nevertheless, the kingdom is *God's*, and its presence and manifestation are divinely initiated, thereby occasioning moments for God's followers to experience such affections as glory, joy, or hope when miracles and signs are on display but also negative or troubling sentiments such as ambiguity, tension, confusion, or frustration when they fail to see God's activity or understand the rationale behind God's purposes. The task at hand is to determine what features of eschatological expectation are reflective of God's own work through the Spirit and what has been misconstrued by overzealous Pentecostals who had a penchant to locate themselves at the cusp of cosmic fulfillment. Without a kind of intentional and patient negotiation of eschatological expectation – in other words, without sensibilities and practices that fit under the practice-orientation of 'waiting' – Pentecostal zeal has the potential of being diminished or altered, and such developments could potentially corrupt the role eschatology ought to play in the worship of an epicletic community. These circumstances raise the overarching question: How should Pentecostals live in the 'already-not yet' tension now that the sense of eschatological immediacy has dissipated with time? Or another way of stating the question: How should Pentecostals 'wait' or 'tarry' in light of unfulfilled eschatological expectation?

---

[12] Frank Macchia, 'The Time is Near! Or, Is It? Dare We Abandon Our Eschatological Expectation?', *Pneuma* 25 (2003), p. 161.

One strategy for negotiating this eschatological tension is the Christian virtue of patience. Despite the diverse tendencies current Pentecostals have inherited from their forebears, a salutary understanding of the 'not yet' aspect of the eschatological dyad would strengthen Pentecostal eschatological resolve so that immediate fulfillment is not cast as a necessary feature of Pentecostal identity more generally and Pentecostal mission and practice particularly. This kind of strengthening and emboldening is needed since Pentecostalism has and continues to undergo various aspects of institutionalization, and the pressures that come with that process have a way of not only 'routinizing charisma' but also of reifying or calcifying themes and motifs that complicate outward and internal negotiation and bequeathal. In other words, the 'already' aspect of eschatological self-understanding that has functioned in the minds of Pentecostals for so long has been exhausted and requires reconfiguration in light of the movement's institutionalization on the American scene. A complementary feature of this identity negotiation would help Pentecostals 'wait' in faithfulness for their soon-coming King in the midst of hardships, suffering, and loss. Such a move would help Pentecostals strike a better balance so that they can continue to be an expectant people without becoming overly frustrated or disappointed. As the matter stands now, Pentecostalism's eschatological self-understanding has been suspended or abandoned because its framing has been unsupportable over time; therefore, a retrieval of the Christian virtue of patience may help rehabilitate the role of eschatology within Pentecostal identity negotiation.

1. The Tradition of Patience: Tertullian

Patience is a long-running theme throughout Christian antiquity. As understood as a virtue of the Christian life, patience has served an important function in Christian reflection as a vital check to eschatological expectation and as a resource of hope within a myriad of challenging and difficult contexts. Therefore, its role within Christian construals of quotidian living has been important and longstanding.

Early Christian reflection on patience culminated with the work of Tertullian, a figure whom Pentecostals extol for his charismatic exuberance in light of his eventual association with the Montanist movement. Ironically, Tertullian had no patience for philosophizing in Christian theology and showed a flair for hyperbole in opposing those whom he deemed in error. He is not a figure one would naturally associate with patience given his polemical writings and his attitudes and dispositions on display therein. And yet Tertullian extolled the value of Christian patience in a work devoted singularly to the theme. The irony was not lost on Tertullian himself when he remarks, 'So I, most miserable, ever sick with the heats of *im*patience, must of necessity sigh after, and invoke, and persistently plead for, that health of patience which I possess not'.[13] Tertullian was well aware he was impatient and that his life did not correspond fully to the embodiment of the virtue of patience that he knew to be proper, yet he recognized that reflection on divine patience served as a solace for his understanding and continual growth in the gospel.

In *Of Patience* Tertullian proceeds in a manner similar to some of his other theological proposals: He begins with reflection on God and then moves to the human situation so that, in this particular instance, God is highlighted as the ultimate exemplar of patience for creatures to imitate. The matter is a keen one from the divine perspective: In relation to the world that God created, God endures the rejection of many, the disobedience of others, and in the process disparages God's own self by allowing a rebellious and insolent creation to stand. In fact, God continues in holy and perfect patience despite occasions of disbelief among those who cannot fathom why God is not more active or 'impatient' with the problems and suffering of the world: God often suffers rejection on the basis of those who in 'righteous anger' cannot tolerate the existence of a good divinity in light of all that is experienced within the creaturely realm. That God would allow a creation to reject Godself on the basis of the longsuffering that God displays in relation to a hurting and broken world indicates, at least from God's side, the importance that the divine patience must exercise in the ways God rules and orders the universe.

Naturally, the most indicative expression of God's patience within the economy is the life and work of Christ. Whereas many of

---

[13] Tertullian, *Of Patience*, I. In what follows, the translations of patristic sources, unless otherwise stated, are taken from the ANF and NPF (First Series) editions published by Hendrickson.

his contemporaries wanted to emphasize the deeds of Christ on earth, Tertullian notes the events and circumstances of Christ's life, which show that Christ indeed endured with great patience those who met, followed, tortured, and even killed him. The godly long-suffering on display in macrocosmic perspective in terms of God's providential care for the world is seen particularly in the way Christ led his singular, mortal life. Both vantage points display a God who refuses to control instrumentally and overdeterminatively God's creation; at the heart of both instances is the great reversal implied by the power that exists in weakness.

As for the role godly patience plays in the life of the believer, Tertullian makes an ingenious case for the claim that every sin is ascribable to impatience, and for this reason, the deficiency of patience in the Christian life is detrimental to Christian discipleship.[14] Patience breeds and vivifies humility, obedience, faith, charity, and mercy, while impatience promotes the opposite vices and behaviors, and as such, impatience provides the dispositional and attitudinal bedrock for outwardly detectable sin. Tertullian raises the example of Abraham for a positive exemplification of holy patience, but a case could be made from both sides of the matter: The father of the faith showed a lack of patience when he deceived Pharaoh with a lie about Sarai in Genesis 12; nevertheless, as Tertullian points out, Abraham grew to be a figure of great patience, as the *akedah* of Genesis 22 shows.

Impatience fosters possessiveness and blurs mourning or loss with covetousness. Patience, conversely, recognizes the giftedness and gratuity of all things, that what one has ultimately has been given. Succinctly stated, impatience derails the Christian life to its core because it transfigures the human need for meaning and order into an idolatrous, anthropocentric form. The appropriation of divine patience by the faithful, conversely, is a precondition for a life of epicletic and doxological faithfulness. As Tertullian states, 'For where God is, there too is His foster-child, namely Patience. Whence God's Spirit descends, then Patience accompanies Him indivisibly'.[15] A patient church then is a Spirit-imbued church. The longsuffering Spirit generates longsuffering Spirit-bearers.

---

[14] Tertullian, *Of Patience*, V.
[15] Tertullian, *Of Patience*, XV.

2. The Tradition of Patience: Additional Sources

In addition to Tertullian's early voice, other theologians throughout Christianity's long history have found it appropriate and helpful to comment on Christian patience. One example would be Cyprian. Reminiscent of his fellow Carthagite, Cyprian asks in contrast to the philosophical espousal of patience: 'For whence can he be either wise or patient, who has neither known the wisdom nor the patience of God?'[16] In other words, patience is a function of knowing God, who is the true and only source of patience. As Cyprian remarks, 'From Him patience begins; from Him its glory and its dignity take their rise. The origin and greatness of patience proceed from God as its author'.[17] Living patiently reflects the Sermon on the Mount and implies obedience to the love commandments of being perfected in imitation of Christ. 'Even he is made alive by Christ's blood', Cyprian writes, 'who has shed Christ's blood. Such and so great is the patience of Christ'.[18] Furthermore, Cyprian argues that patience is not simply a matter of obedience but of survival for the Christian: 'Nor can there be supplied any consolations to those that sweat and toil other than patience; which consolations, while in this world they are fit and necessary for all men, are especially so for us who are more shaken by the siege of the devil, who, daily standing in the battle-field, are wearied with the wrestlings of an inveterate and skillful enemy'.[19] Cyprian recognizes that the Christian life is one of afflictions and sorrows, and fostering patience is a means by which to resist and endure the antagonisms that come with living in the 'time between the times'.

Augustine also contributes to the subject in his treatise *On Patience*, affirming that patience is a great gift from God bestowed on believers. Augustine asserts that God is impassible, that is, God does not suffer, and yet Augustine whole-heartedly recognizes that the 'long-suffering' God is ineffably and mysteriously patient, just as he is wondrously 'jealous without any darkening of spirit, wroth without any perturbation, pitiful without any pain', and repentant without having to be set right.[20] Augustine highlights patience as a

---

[16] Cyprian, *On the Advantage of Patience*, II.
[17] Cyprian, *On the Advantage of Patience*, III.
[18] Cyprian, *On the Advantage of Patience*, VIII.
[19] Cyprian, *On the Advantage of Patience*, XII.
[20] Augustine, *On Patience*, I.

resource for the persecuted and suffering church as it attempts to endure the trials and tribulations that inevitably accompany Christ-followers in a broken world.

Thomas Aquinas extends Augustine's arguments in an article on patience in the *Summa Theologiae*. Moving from Augustine's passing reference to patience as a 'virtue of the mind', Thomas notes that patience is necessary for reason not to be impeded by the sorrow in the world.[21] But Thomas goes on to locate patience as a function of charity, the chief of the theological virtues. In this way, patience is a function of grace while at the same time it can retain some of its qualities as a virtue. Thomas concludes his discussion of patience by comparing it to longanimity or longsuffering. Thomas notes that patience endures certain evils for the sake of good, but over time the endurance becomes more difficult; the postponement of hope causes sadness, but patience helps one in the endurance of sorrows.[22] Aquinas' commentary on Tully is enlightening:

> For this reason Tully in defining patience, says that *patience is the voluntary and prolonged endurance of arduous and difficult things for the sake of virtue or profit*. By saying *arduous* he refers to constancy in the good; when he says *difficult* he refers to the grievousness of evil, which is the proper object of patience; and by adding *continued* or *long lasting*, he refers to longanimity, in so far as it has something in common with patience.[23]

For our purposes, the last figure worth considering is John Wesley. As a clergyman in the Church of England, Wesley was steeped in the traditions of the church fathers and appropriated their theological views in the development of his own theology of holiness and Christian perfection. Taking Jas 1.4 as a guiding text, Wesley in a sermon related to the theme considers patience in light of the onslaught of trials and temptations in this life. He defines patience not as a heathen virtue but as 'a gracious temper wrought in the heart of a believer by the power of the Holy Ghost' and 'a disposition to suffer whatever pleases God, in the manner and for the time that pleases him'.[24] Through the use of the language of 'tempers', Wesley

---

[21] *ST*, II-II, q.136, a.1.
[22] *ST*, II-II, q.136, a. 5.
[23] *ST*, II-II, q.136, a. 5 (emphasis indicates quoted material).
[24] John Wesley, 'On Patience', III, p. 171.

is reiterating that patience is a religious affection, a work of God that takes place in the heart but nevertheless requires enactment. Patience leads to the fruits of peace and joy in the midst of sufferings, and these difficulties and their associated acts of enduring them work in shaping Christian character, in helping believers grow in holiness.

3. Pentecostal Appropriation of Patience and Eschatological Hypertrophy

The voices of these Christian thinkers are suggestive for the task of reconsidering the value of eschatological expectation. One could draw several points from these noted figures and their intentional reflection on the virtue of patience for precisely such a task. As these figures repeatedly note, patience is a gift from God that can only come from God since God is its ultimate exemplar. True patience is neither humanly achieved nor deceptively fabricated independent of God's ongoing work of rehabilitating and sustaining God's people. Only God is the source and end of true patience, and true patience is without question needed to sustain the community of faith in the trials of this life. In other words, godly patience is a function of 'abiding in the vine' that is the sustaining and empowering presence of the triune God.

God's patience becomes the Christian's patience when it is embodied, attended to, and exercised as an affection or temper that bears fruit. But also, the consideration of patience as a virtue is helpful in that such language (as noted earlier in this study) suggests 'habituation' and 'performance' in the Christian life. Practices and models of patience are needed so that the patient character of a community is on display for both adherent and interested onlooker to see. The opportunity for it to be exercised and meaningfully operative within the collective life of the epicletic community is precisely in times of hardship: Patience is an indispensable feature of the church's christoform identity when it faces both persecution and sorrow, for it can serve as a resource for sustained confrontation and resistance to evil in the world. Patience is crucial when the 'not yet' aspect of kingdom living is outright and burdensome for communal life. In fact, as the implications of the above authors and their works would suggest, a faithful community cannot sustain its life in faithfulness to God apart from habitually 'waiting'. Outside of the virtue of patience, Christian fellowship may, in the face of persecution, resort to either 'responding in kind' (and so offering retaliatory actions that are inconsistent with the life of Jesus) or choosing defeat at the hands of the enemy (either by way of dissolution or capitulation). As the incarnation (with all the suffering and anguish that such an act implied) was indicative of godly patience, so the suffering of trials by the body of Christ can indicate a cruciform hopefulness that awaits ultimate eschatological redemption and healing. Such moments can be the occasion for the most genuine and compelling expressions of the truthfulness of the gospel since they would occur when something is truly and obviously at stake.

Pentecostals would do well to learn from past articulations of Christian patience, for the complications resulting from their 'sanctified impatience' have started to take their toll on the movement's theological coherence and its current-day identity and practices. Specifically, American Pentecostals have capitulated to some degree in terms of their call to be an epicletic community because of their quest for public respectability. The consequences of such a course of action are dire, for as Augustine relevantly notes in *De Patientia*: 'The patience of a man ... is understood to be that by which we tolerate evil things with an even mind, that we may not with a mind uneven desert good things, through which we may arrive at better'.[25] Augustine suggests that patience is inherent to the practice of resisting evil and appreciating the good, making it a virtue that serves well in the long-term faithfulness of any person or group over time. Pentecostalism, therefore, is at a place in its history where it needs to draw from the deep wells of the Christian faith, ones in which theologians of godly patience can maybe shed light on the particularities of Pentecostalism's eschatological self-understanding, in order to ameliorate the negative effects of impatient urgency in Pentecostal identity and practice.

For instance, Pentecostal impatience has inspired eschatological impatience by occasioning the conception of divine and human activity in the world in such a way that a theological understanding of the economy of salvation is truncated. Specifically, Faupel notes

---

[25] Augustine, *On Patience*, II.

that many early Pentecostals believed not only that Jesus' return was imminent but that their evangelistic practices could in fact *hasten* Christ's return. Though perhaps naïve and prone to colonial ideology, early Pentecostals believed that Christ's second coming would be preceded, and so could be prompted, by the preaching of the gospel unto the ends of the earth.[26] For all the 'escapist' tendencies within Pentecostalism, on this point they tended to be quite optimistic about how human efforts could influence salvation history to reach its denouement. D.J. Wilson suggests as much when he notes that some early Pentecostals believed their efforts could '*facilitate* [Jesus'] return'.[27]

The perceived possibility of hastening the second coming is brimming with theological difficulties, not only for what it suggests about divine-human interaction in the economy of salvation history but also in relation to the kind of expectancy that is envisioned, one that can lead to frustration over the course of time. In the first place, Pentecostals have tended in large degree to a kind of Arminian formulation of the grace-free will debate *vis-à-vis* Wesley; therefore, much of the revivalist camp-meeting ethos emphasized the value of human freedom, choice, enactment, and embodiment, even at the risk of blurring divine-human distinctions. Through practices such as miracle-working, healing, and prophecy, Pentecostals have operated with a strong conviction that because of God's empowering work on their lives and in their communities, they have an important role on the stage of cosmic history. Yet this sense of empowerment brings with it the lurking temptation to assume that what occurs in this world (including those enactments of possibilities by human agents) directly influences features of the heavenly realm. This tendency has the potential to displace divine

---

[26] D. William Faupel, *The Everlasting Gospel*, pp. 21-22. The logic worked well for thinking of tongues as xenolalia, as Charles Parham at one point did. As Althouse notes,

> Parham believed that since the coming of Christ was going to occur in his lifetime, there was an urgent need to evangelize the world. The intensity of missions thinking, an intensity forged in the belief that preaching the gospel to the whole world was the last requirement to be fulfilled before Christ would return, provided a utilitarian function for tongue speaking as an empowerment for Christian service (Althouse, *Spirit of the Last Days*, pp. 26-27).

[27] Wilson, 'Eschatology, Pentecostal Perspectives on', *DPCM*, pp. 604-605, (emphasis added).

sovereignty and freedom through an anthropocentric self-willing, thereby diminishing the complexity of the relationship between God and God's creation. In other words, the elevation of the human role at the cost of the divine freedom and majesty tragically overlooks human finitude and sinfulness. Within this scenario, the running risk for Pentecostals is a self-originated sense of theological importance and triumphalism (and correlatively, a sense of despair when the expected outcomes do not materialize).

Perhaps illustrative of this theological danger is the assumption that one can expect a miraculous intervention of healing or blessing if one fulfills an assumed set of requirements. Yet, with such a logic in place, one may suffer disappointment when the expected miracle does not occur. Overlooked in this construal and expectation set is the role of God's sovereignty and freedom. The theological risk of ritualizing God's activity according to human 'faith requirements' is that it represents an attempt to control God and to elevate the role of human activity.[28] Perhaps most indicative of the theological risks involved are cases when human suffering is blamed on the sufferers because, it is assumed, they do not have enough faith or are hiding unconfessed sin. Certainly, one does not want to downplay the miraculous, which can be an occasion for revealing God's gracious character and the prompting of both joy and assurance among believers. When the miraculous does occur (and Pentecostals are quite prone to emphasize such moments), the divine-human logic at play, whatever it happens to be, can continue to be held quite happily. But how do Pentecostals theologically explain the absence of divine miracles or blessings (instances that Pentecostals often quickly pass by or avoid)? On too many occasions, fault is ascribed to the seeker and alternative explanations are overlooked, especially the possibility that God's ways are mysterious and often different from

---

[28] Of course, not all Pentecostal theologies of healing are prone to make healing a somewhat 'automatic' event, but enough of them do that they can be situated between the extremes of 'divine faithfulness' and 'divine freedom.' See Henry H. Knight, III, 'God's Faithfulness and God's Freedom', *Journal of Pentecostal Theology* 2 (1993), pp. 65-89. On the former side of the continuum, people believe God has promised blessings or pronounced laws which come into effect only when believers appropriately and sufficiently believe. Within such understandings, healing occurs on the basis of one's faith more so than God's timing or sovereign will, and such postures define faith as 'trusting in God's promises in Scripture rather than trusting in God' (p. 69). This scenario reduces relationality (a key component of spirituality) to technique.

humanity's.[29] Such closures can only destroy the epicletic community from within; rather than being imaginatively and patiently epicletic, such a fellowship conflates divine power with human power,
thereby leading to the gravest of theological sins: idolatry.

The unfulfilled expectation of miracles by individual adherents is
but a microcosmic analogy of the greater problem of Pentecostal
eschatological expectancy today. Past expectation of the immediacy
of Jesus' second coming and the fervor this created are logically
precarious when they are associated with the assumption that human creatures can force God's hand. As such, many early Pentecostals mistakenly believed that their work could hasten Jesus' return if
all the signs of the last days, especially the preaching of the gospel
to all nations, were fulfilled. However, because of their eschatological impatience, Pentecostals have all-too-often allowed their hope
to shift from fervency to cynicism, contributing to the diminution
of an eschatologically self-understood ethos in many established
Pentecostal circles today.

4. Reconfiguring the Eschatological Form

Pentecostal warrants for evangelism and mission were eschatologically awry in a number of ways, but their eschatological fervor was
not simply prompted by a mythos of sorts but also by the real and
tangible experience of God's inbreaking kingdom within their
doxological practices. In this regard, the matter is more complex
than to say simply that early Pentecostals were mistaken in what
they believed about the end times. Admittedly, certain details they
promoted about the unfolding of cosmic history were wrong (as
time has shown), and their penchant for overusing the Apocalypse
was indicative at times of their nascent capitulation to fundamentalist dispensationalism,[30] but their expectation of the eschatological

---

[29] In surveying the beliefs of the charismatic Agnes Sanford, Knight remarks,
'For Sanford, when a person we pray for is not healed it is usually due to our
being an inadequate channel of God's healing energy ... This does not mean we
cannot be healed by our own prayers. But if we are not, again the problem is with
us' (Knight, 'God's Faithfulness and God's Freedom', p. 71). Such a logic per-
vades Pentecostal settings as well.

[30] Of course, not all early Pentecostals adhered to a dispensational eschatology. On this, see Larry R. McQueen, *Toward a Pentecostal Eschatology: Discerning the
Way Forward* (JPTSup 39; Blandford Forum, UK: Deo Publishing, 2012).

coming of God was theologically feasible in that eschatology is at the heart of what it means to be the people of God directed outward in accordance with the Great Commission. If the church lives 'between the times' in that Pentecost is precisely the inbreaking of God's kingdom on earth, then Pentecostals have sensed this eschatological impulse more powerfully than many since that understanding led them to take action.

Therefore, early Pentecostals were mistaken to think that in their historical lifetimes they would see and perhaps even hasten Christ's return, but their conviction that they could hope to see their soon-coming King still applies; their hope, as all Christian hope, begins and ends with God. Yes, many of their illustrations and metaphors for interpreting history are less persuasive now with the passing of time, but the Christian reading of history continues to have one end, goal, and consummation. Admittedly, early Pentecostals may have aggrandized their role and place within the divine economy (and such attitudes and their concomitant effects should be occasions for confession and repentance), but their claims stemmed from the deep conviction that God was actively working in their lives and communities in powerful and wondrous ways. They may have gone to the extreme of elevating themselves too highly, but early Pentecostals were surely right to emphasize the cosmic implications of Pentecost for the creation as it is now understood in a post-resurrection state.

Expressed pithily, early Pentecostals were wrong about some of the details but were faithful generally to expect and live in light of the eschatological kingdom. The task for contemporary Pentecostals, and especially the Pentecostal academy in aid to the subtradition as a whole, is to preserve those positive features of early Pentecostal expectancy without succumbing to end-time scenarios based upon theologically aggrandizing rationales and problematic operational assumptions. If contemporary Pentecostals are to live in light of this vision, then like Tertullian their call is nothing less than to wait patiently for a patient God in spite of their creaturely impatience. In applying what Cyprian suggests, one could say that the patience Pentecostals are to cultivate can only come from God, and such cultivation ought to be undertaken with passion, commitment, and yes, a certain dialectic that includes both restlessness and equanimity. Such a strategy means that God's tarrying (that is, God's patience) is not eschatological misfortune or tragedy but a reflection of the divine perseverance stemming from the sovereign God in whom Christians trust. These points can be held alongside the conviction that 'what their eyes have seen' and 'their hands have touched' really constitute the inbreaking kingdom of God. To summarize the dialectic, Pentecostals, as all Christians, *need God in order to wait on God in hopeful and patient expectation; they need to abide in God as they wait for God.*

5. Practicing Patience

To this end, Pentecostals can move forward in reconfiguring their particular species of expectancy through a multi-tiered process, one in which patience is practiced and cultivated through specific activities. A number of possibilities could be proposed here, but some seem especially pivotal in light of how the movement has taken shape thus far.

First, the function of lament is worth pursuing within Pentecostal communal life.[31] In acknowledging that their expectancy has not been fulfilled – that Christ has not returned as expected or that one is not healed or apparently shown blessing – Pentecostals can recognize in concrete circumstances the promise of hope. Admittedly, Christ's tarrying has allowed suffering to continue, but one could argue that Pentecostals have avoided talk of lament in their public pronouncements for fear that doing so would be perceived as a sign of inadequate faith.[32] Of course, Pentecostal neglect of lament is but symptomatic of the church as a whole, but especially in light of

---

[31] Pentecostals have begun to work with the topic of lament, notably, see Scott Ellington, *Risking Truth: Reshaping the World through Prayers of Lament* (Eugene: Pickwick, 2008). However, connections between lament and the Pentecostal ethos are not made in this work and are pressing in contemporary Pentecostal theology.

[32] Kimberly Alexander notes how controversial it was for early Pentecostal publications to include obituaries. Certain strands of Pentecostalism, like the Finished Work camp, avoided obituaries altogether, and groups that included them, such as Wesleyan Pentecostals, did so by emphasizing that in death believers were victorious and 'going home', occasions that should inspire joy and worship. See Kimberly E. Alexander, *Pentecostal Healing: Models in Theology and Practice* (JPTSup 29; Blandford Forum: Deo, 2006), pp. 208-209. Given the absence of lament themes among Pentecostals, one wonders if lament practices, as biblically sound as they are, have been avoided because they are understood to betray what are deemed to be vital features of the movement.

the challenges American Pentecostalism faces, lament could in fact be a way toward renewal of eschatological expectancy because at its core such a process promotes genuineness and truthfulness since it recognizes the vulnerable and precarious state in which the epicletic community lives.[33] The desire for a soon-coming King and his reign is both prompted by signs of that kingdom but also hampered by the reality of its still awaited fulfillment. Therefore, Pentecostals ought to realize that being a community of hope implies being a patient people who participate in the *koinonia* of one another's sufferings, hoping for their soon-returning Lord in the midst (rather than in spite) of their plight. As Keith Warrington notes, 'The recognition of the place of suffering in Pentecostal theology needs to be redeemed as an integral aspect of an authentic spirituality that acknowledges the value of suffering in the life of the believer and does not simply attempt to exclude it or assume that its presence is intrinsically illegitimate'.[34]

In cultivating the practice of lament, Pentecostals can appropriate the logic of Wesley's 'means of grace' in such a fashion that it can cultivate expectancy so that it does not require immediate fulfillment for it to be available. The practice of patience in the Pentecostal context would mean 'tarrying' and attending to that which believers can so that they recognize that at times God discloses God's self powerfully but at others (perhaps in most cases) God remains hidden. Either way, steadfastness in waiting must be a vital feature of a Pentecostal spirituality so that circumstances do not become harmfully determinative of the quality of Pentecostal life.[35] To extrapolate from Wesley in this particular matter of eschatological expectancy, one can say that Pentecostals must attend to the

---

[33] Walter Brueggemann has done much to retrieve the theme of lament for the contemporary life of the church based on his reading of the Psalms. In his view, avoiding lament implies the 'loss of *genuine covenant interaction*' as well as '*the stifling of the question of theodicy*' (Walter Brueggemann, *The Psalms and the Life of Faith*, ed. Patrick D. Miller [Minneapolis: Fortress, 1995], pp. 102 and 104 [emphases in original]). When lament is seen as impossible or unfaithful, the harshness of reality is minimized or explained away. As the Psalms prove, lament is an important part of a vital, engaged, fruitful, and honest faith. I pursue this matter more extensively in Daniel Castelo, *Theological Theodicy* (Eugene: Cascade: 2012).

[34] Keith Warrington, *Pentecostal Theology: A Theology of Encounter* (London: T & T Clark, 2008), p. 303.

[35] For a contribution within the vein of Wesleyan-Pentecostal spirituality, see Henry H. Knight, III, 'From Aldersgate to Azusa', *Journal of Pentecostal Theology* 8 (1996), pp. 82-98.

means of grace patiently and consistently regardless of whether they see God moving. The kinds of attitudes and the form of resiliency fostered through such practices would help them in the long-run become a people who can sustain the pressures of both persecution and accommodation with a Spirit-shaped and suffering-tested resolve that could make possible the preservation and transmission of their Spirit-prompted intuitions across generations.

Finally, Pentecostals would do well to operate with a reverent sense of the mysteries of God in such a way that patience takes the form of resisting explanation when one does not understand or when a certain expectation has not been fulfilled, whether it be the second coming more generally or any specific request for healing, blessing, or the like. As the reader probably notes through this point and the last, the reframing of Pentecostal eschatological expectation is significantly tied to the formulation of some kind of practical theodicy.[36] But the matter runs deeper than simply the required reconfiguration of the relationship between God's character (including God's longsuffering) and the evil that exists in the world; it also includes a reformulation of the way Pentecostals go about the theological task more generally in light of their doxological experiences.

Pentecostal belief in the immediacy of God's presence in doxological space and mode carries with it the pressure to explain God's apparent lack of action. Pentecostals, compelled as they are to make the theo-logic of their altar encounters available and coherent to themselves and others, have all too easily made the leap to clarify or elaborate God's purposes in unbridled and rushed ways. The only way apparently out of such a conundrum involves a theological reconfiguration of both God's manifest and hidden work. Both require a re-enchantment and maybe even a fearful appreciation of the divine mystery. Pentecostals on the whole celebrate God's unpredictability, that God through God's Spirit can appear and work in unanticipated ways; that sensibility needs to be more fully orbed, however, in that God's unpredictability cuts both ways. No matter

---

[36] Another way of stating the matter is to suggest that Pentecostals ought to evolve into a post-theodical people who approach evil and suffering not via a cold, syllogistic, hard rationalism, but through practices of resistance, endurance, and dispositions of compassion and empathy.

how many prayers, vigils, and fasts, the desired outcome (from the human side of the matter) may not occur.

Such framing within the holy mysteries suggests that expectancy has a similar shape to faith, one that operates precisely in patience for its eventual resolution. Some mysteries remain, and God is the only one who will make them known in God's own time. In the meantime, the role of believers is to endure the 'cognitive dissonance' and tests of faith that stem from both God's visibility *and* hiddenness, from God's work in the form of 'signs and wonders' *and* God's tarrying. Rather than avoiding or silencing suffering, Pentecostals need to recognize that part of the Spirit's work includes the practical dimension of helping the faithful overcome and endure both suffering and evil as they patiently wait for the unfolding of God's eschatological reign; it also means that the Spirit's work implies that certain forays into theological speculation can only hurt the faithful in the long-run. Certain hypotheses, end-times scenarios, and theological explanations and rationales simply are unnecessary and potentially even spiritually derailing for the faithful at large. The gratuity on display in the divine self-disclosure is both sufficiently generative and enchanting for the epicletic community to continue on in its task of 'abiding' and 'waiting'. Embodying patience means pursuing a species of theology that is more conceptually humble and austere, less verbose and explanatory, and more attendant to the practical and spiritual needs of the faithful.

6. Conclusion

To conclude, Pentecostals are at an important juncture in our history. We have been forced to reconsider our origins and mission in light of God's patience; in other words, we have been forced to wait in unexpected ways. Our waiting is centered on God's waiting just as our expectancy is a result of God's free and gracious activity in our midst. In both cases, God's role drives both the possibilities and limits of what can be said and imagined. But given their exuberance regarding the way God has worked in their midst, Pentecostals have traditionally had few resources in narrating theologically God's hiddenness in the midst of God's revealedness, God's apparent absence in addition to God's manifest presence. Theologically, this growing awareness of the need to be a patient people may be strange and unexpected for Pentecostals, but it certainly is not improper, and it may even be timely given where the subtradition currently finds itself. As with expectancy, so with waiting: As a people of God, Pentecostals and all Christians receive their hope and vitality from the God of Abraham, Isaac, and Jacob; the God revealed in the life of Jesus Christ; and the God who continues to wait patiently as a sign of grace. The epicletic community can abide in and wait for God with hope-filled expectancy even in the midst of persecutions and hardships, for its vision of how things are is thoroughly inflected and configured by how they will be … in God's own time and way.

CONCLUSION

The argument in this volume has been constructive with an eye to being reparative as well. The assumption at play is that if Pentecostalism is a spirituality, it needs to be explicitly intentional in how it negotiates embodiment and performance in a theological way. Because of a deficiency in this regard over the years, Pentecostalism has changed dramatically in its established contexts: Revivalism has become less and less appealing as a 'way of being church', but the alternative on the horizon, a generic Evangelicalism, is in strong tension with the Pentecostal ethos on a number of levels. The pressures from both within and without have made Pentecostal identity contested and in some sense tenuous. As a result, the ethical-theological task is pressing within this subtradition of Christianity.

By way of concluding this text, let me summarize some of the most generative and suggestive claims made herein that seek to address this condition.

The ethical-theological task within Pentecostalism is best understood in terms of moral theology rather than Christian ethics. This argument is based on the prior assumption that Pentecostalism is best understood as a practiced spirituality in which God is the beginning and end not only of intellectual inquiry but human selves in all of their particularity and embeddedness. Such privileging honors some of the pre-modern tendencies inherent to Pentecostalism all the while recognizing that these are picked up in a modern and late-modern situation. Within this rubric of a spirituality, Pentecostalism represents not so much a 'religious persuasion' or 'point of view' but a way of being and participating in the world. Pentecostalism in its essence is a 'take on life' that presses through some of the most prevalent assumptions of Christianity within the Western intellectual climate.

In particular, Pentecostalism privileges worship as a way of securing authority and truth claims; doxology is a modality of knowing and being, and as such, this text has typified Pentecostalism as an 'epicletic community'. The former term in the phrase has been chosen because it operates in a synergistically indeterminate situation of God permeating all things and yet human selves recognizing, naming, and living into that reality. The latter term, 'community', was included because Pentecostalism is best understood as an ethos more so than a privatized or individualistic concern.

From these primordial assumptions, the text moved to consider the practice-orientations of 'abiding' and 'waiting', not only because they are biblical motifs of the peregrinating Christian community but also because they represented doxologically related dispositions that located a community within a broader reality. The Pentecostal fellowship is to abide in Christ through the power of the Spirit and to wait for the Lord in the power and comfort of the second Paraclete. Again, these tropes are synergistically indeterminate because they involve human selves but do so in ways that recognize the preeminence and prevenient role of the transcendent and mysterious Trinity, the God whom Pentecostals and other Christians seek to encounter and be transformed by in the totality of their lives.

Within the horizons of 'abiding' and 'waiting', the text moved to consider the affections and virtues as viable ethical models within Christian moral reflection. The case was made that within the form of Pentecostal being-in-the-world, the gestures of 'from above to below' and 'from below to above' require some kind of conceptual recognition. Affections are especially amenable to a characterization and formation that are said to take place 'from above', for Pentecostals have a penchant to emphasize the doxological encounter with the Holy Trinity and all of the changes that can come about from such an event. At stake in this discussion was a vision of normativity for Pentecostal affectivity, one that locates affectivity within the broader purposes of God's work in the world. Virtues, on the other hand, take time and effort; in short, they require habituation, and these too can be depicted through a grace-laden understanding, one that presses the continuity between the triune God's work of redemption *and creation*. With virtues can come the emphases of working out one's own salvation and of purifying and making oneself amenable to divine promptings. In both cases, the form of Christ's life is both apprehended and in some sense realized through the continual work of the Spirit in and through the life of the faithful.

Finally, the work moved to consider two areas of theological-ethical consideration especially important to Pentecostals that need reconfiguration and address. The first matter relates to the rehabilitation of the doctrinal-experiential locus of sanctification, one that has waned and been rendered largely incoherent within Pentecostalism because of a number of pressures upon the revivalist-crisis model of spiritual experience. The second topic under scrutiny was Pentecostal eschatological expectation, one that has suffered significantly as generations have come and gone within the Pentecostal fold. The practice-orientations of abiding and waiting as well as the interplay of affections and virtues contributed to a recasting of these central concerns related to Pentecostal ethics.

Much work continues to be needed within this subtradition in relation to theological-ethical themes. My longing is that this volume helps spawn a renewal within established Pentecostalism, both in retrieving important features of the past but also in inspiring an imaginative hope about the future. In short, I wish that a 'sanctified eccentricity' continues to be a mark of Pentecostalism wherever it is to be found, a species of eccentricity that is driven by an insatiable desire and passion to see, befriend, and delight in the triune God of Christian confession.

BIBLIOGRAPHY

Alexander, Kimberly E., *Pentecostal Healing: Models in Theology and Practice* (JPTSup 29; Blandford Forum: Deo, 2006).

Alexander, Paul, *Peace to War: Shifting Allegiances in the Assemblies of God* (Telford: Cascadia, 2009).

Althouse, Peter, *The Spirit of the Last Days: Pentecostal Eschatology in Conversation with Jürgen Moltmann* (JPTSup 25; London: T & T Clark, 2003).

Anderson, Robert Mapes, *Vision of the Disinherited: The Making of American Pentecostalism* (Oxford: Oxford University Press, 1979).

Aquinas, Thomas, *Summa theologiae* (trans. Fathers of the English Dominican Province; Allen: Christian Classics, 1948).

Aristotle, *Nicomachean Ethics* (trans. Terence Irvin; Indianapolis: Hackett Publishing, 1999).

Augustine, *Confessions* (trans. Maria Boulding; New York: Vintage, 1997).

Barth, Karl, *Church Dogmatics, III/4* (eds. G.W. Bromiley and T.F. Torrance; Edinburgh: T & T Clark, 1961).

Beaman, Jay, *Pentecostal Pacifism: The Origin, Development, and Rejection of Pacific Belief among the Pentecostals* (Hillsboro: Center for Mennonite Brethren Studies, 1989).

Begbie, Jeremy, *Theology, Music and Time* (Cambridge: Cambridge University Press, 2000).

Brueggemann, Walter, *The Psalms and the Life of Faith* (ed. Patrick D. Miller; Minneapolis: Fortress Press, 1995).

Buber, Martin, *I and Thou* (Edinburgh: T & T Clark, 1937).

Buckley, James J. and David S. Yeago (eds.), *Knowing the Triune God: The Work of the Spirit in the Practices of the Church* (Grand Rapids: Eerdmans, 2001).

Burgess, Stanley (ed.), *New International Dictionary of Pentecostal and Charismatic Movements* (Grand Rapids: Zondervan, rev. and updated edn, 2002)

—(ed.), *Encyclopedia of Pentecostal and Charismatic Christianity* (New York: Routledge, 2006).

Cahill, Lisa, *Love Your Enemies* (Minneapolis: Fortress, 1994).

Castelo, Daniel, 'Canonical Theism as Ecclesial and Ecumenical Resource', *Pneuma* 33 (2011), pp. 370-89.

—'Holiness *Simpliciter*: A Wesleyan Engagement and Proposal in Light of John Webster's Trinitarian Dogmatics of Holiness', *Wesleyan Theological Journal* 47 (2012), forthcoming.

—*Theological Theodicy* (Eugene: Cascade, 2012).

—(ed.), *Holiness as a Liberal Art* (Eugene: Pickwick, forthcoming).

Cessario, Romanus, *Introduction to Moral Theology* (Washington, DC: Catholic University of America Press, 2001).

Clapper, Gregory S., '"True Religion" and the Affections: A Study of John Wesley's Abridgement of Jonathan Edwards' *Treatise on Religious Affections*', *Wesleyan Theological Journal* 19 (1984), pp. 77-89.

—*John Wesley on Religious Affections: His Views on Experience and Emotion and Their Role in the Christian Life and Theology* (Metuchen: Scarecrow, 1989).

—'*Orthokardia*: The Practical Theology of John Wesley's Heart Religion', *Quarterly Review* 10 (1990), pp. 49-66.

—'John Wesley's Theology of the Heart', *Wesleyan Theological Journal* 44 (2009), pp. 94-102.

—*The Renewal of the Heart is the Mission of the Church* (Eugene: Cascade, 2011).

Collins, Kenneth, 'John Wesley's Topography of the Heart: Dispositions, Tempers, and Affections', *Methodist History* 36 (1998), pp. 162-75.

—'Why the Holiness Movement is Dead', *Asbury Theological Journal* 54 (1999), pp. 27-35.

Colón-Emeric, Edgardo A., *Wesley, Aquinas and Christian Perfection: An Ecumenical Dialogue* (Waco: Baylor University Press, 2009).

Congar, Yves, *I Believe in the Holy Spirit* (3 vols.; New York: Crossroad Herder, 2000).

Coulter, Dale, '"Delivered by the Power of God": Toward a Pentecostal Understanding of Salvation', *International Journal of Systematic Theology* 10 (2008), pp. 447-67.

—'Pentecostalism, Mysticism, and Renewal Methodologies', *Pneuma* 33 (2011), pp. 1-4.

Dixon, Thomas, *From Passions to Emotions: The Creation of a Secular Psychological Category* (Cambridge: Cambridge University Press, 2003).

Edwards, Jonathan, *The Works of Jonathan Edwards, volume 2: Religious Affections* (ed. John E. Smith; New Haven: Yale University Press, 1959).

Ellington, Scott, *Risking Truth: Reshaping the World through Prayers of Lament* (Eugene: Pickwick, 2008).

Faupel, D. William, *The Everlasting Gospel: The Significance of Eschatology in the Development of Pentecostal Thought* (JPTSup 10; Sheffield: Sheffield Academic Press, 1996).

Goroncy, Jason, 'The Elusiveness, Loss and Cruciality of Recovered Holiness', *International Journal of Systematic Theology* 10 (2008), pp. 195-209.

Gunton, Colin E. (ed.), *The Cambridge Companion to Christian Doctrine* (Cambridge: Cambridge University Press, 1997).

Hauerwas, Stanley, *The Peaceable Kingdom: A Primer in Christian Ethics* (Notre Dame: University of Notre Dame Press, 1983).

Hauerwas, Stanley and Samuel Wells (eds.), *The Blackwell Companion to Christian Ethics* (Oxford: Blackwell, 2006).

Hollenweger, Walter J., 'The Critical Tradition of Pentecostalism', *Journal of Pentecostal Theology* 1 (1992), pp. 7-17.

Hütter, Reinhard, *Suffering Divine Things: Theology as Church Practice* (Grand Rapids: Eerdmans, 1999).

Jacobsen, Douglas, *Thinking in the Spirit: Theologies of the Early Pentecostal Movement* (Bloomington: Indiana University Press, 2003).

Johns, Cheryl Bridges, 'The Adolescence of Pentecostalism: In Search of a Legitimate Sectarian Identity', *Pneuma* 17 (1995), pp. 3-17.

Johnston, Robert K., L. Gregory Jones, and Jonathan R. Wilson (eds.), *Grace upon Grace: Essays in Honor of Thomas A. Langford* (Nashville: Abingdon, 1999).

Knight, Henry H., III, *The Presence of God in the Christian Life: John Wesley and the Means of Grace* (Metuchen: Scarecrow, 1992).

—'God's Faithfulness and God's Freedom', *Journal of Pentecostal Theology* 2 (1993), pp. 65-89.

—'From Aldersgate to Azusa', *Journal of Pentecostal Theology* 8 (1996), pp. 82-98.

—(ed.), *From Aldersgate to Azusa Street: Wesleyan, Holiness, and Pentecostal Visions of the New Creation* (Eugene: Pickwick, 2010).

Kotva, Joseph J., Jr, *The Christian Case for Virtue Ethics* (Washington, DC: Georgetown University Press, 1996).

Land, Steven J. *Pentecostal Spirituality: A Passion for the Kingdom* (JPTSup 1; Sheffield: Sheffield Academic Press, 1994).

Lash, Nicholas, *Theology on the Way to Emmaus* (Eugene: Wipf and Stock, 2005).

Levison, John R., *'Filled with the Spirit*: A Conversation with Pentecostal and Charismatic Scholars', *Journal of Pentecostal Theology* 20 (2011), pp. 213-31.

—'Recommendations for the Future of Pneumatology', *Pneuma* 33 (2011), pp. 79-93.

Lewis, Paul W., 'A Pneumatological Approach to Virtue Ethics', *Asian Journal of Pentecostal Studies* 1 (1998), pp. 42-61.

Lindbeck, George, *The Nature of Doctrine: Religion and Theology in a Postliberal Age* (Philadelphia: Westminster, 1984).

Long, D. Stephen, *The Goodness of God: Theology, the Church, and Social Order* (Grand Rapids: Brazos, 2001).

—*John Wesley's Moral Theology: The Quest for God and Goodness* (Nashville: Kingswood, 2005).

Macchia, Frank, 'Is Footwashing the Neglected Sacrament?', *Pneuma* 19 (1997), pp. 239-49.

—'The Time is Near! Or, Is It? Dare We Abandon Our Eschatological Expectation?', *Pneuma* 25 (2003), pp. 161-63.

—*Baptized in the Spirit: A Global Pentecostal Theology* (Grand Rapids: Zondervan, 2006).

—'The Spirit of Life and the Spirit of Immortality: An Appreciative Review of Levison's *Filled with the Spirit*', *Pneuma* 33 (2011), pp. 69-78.

MacIntyre, Alasdair, *After Virtue* (Notre Dame: University of Notre Dame Press, 2nd edn, 1984).

Maddox, Randy L. (ed.), *Aldersgate Reconsidered* (Nashville: Kingswood, 1990).

Mattison, William C., III, *Introducing Moral Theology: True Happiness and the Virtues* (Grand Rapids: Brazos, 2008).

McClendon, Jr., William James, *Ethics: Systematic Theology, volume 1* (Nashville: Abingdon, 1986).

McQueen, Larry R., *Toward a Pentecostal Eschatology: Discerning the Way Forward* (JPTSup 39; Blandford Forum, UK: Deo Publishing, 2012).

Melina, Livio, *Sharing in Christ's Virtues: For a Renewal of Moral Theology in Light of Veritatis Splendor* (Washington, DC: Catholic University of America Press, 2001).

Miller, Donald E. and Tetsunao Yamamori, *Global Pentecostalism: The New Face of Christian Social Engagement* (Berkeley: University of California Press, 2007).

Murphy, Nancey, Brad J. Kallenberg, and Mark Thiessen Nation (eds.), *Virtues and Practices in the Christian Tradition: Christian Ethics after MacIntyre* (Harrisburg: Trinity Press International, 1997).

Pinckaers, Servais, 'Virtue is not a Habit', *Cross Currents* 12 (1962), pp. 65-81.

—*The Sources of Christian Ethics* (Washington, DC: Catholic University of America Press, 1995).

—*Morality: The Catholic View* (South Bend: St. Augustine's, 2001).

Poloma, Margaret, *The Assemblies of God at the Crossroads: Charisma and Institutional Dilemmas* (Knoxville: University of Tennessee Press, 1989).

Porter, Jean, *The Recovery of Virtue: The Relevance of Aquinas for Christian Ethics* (Louisville: Westminster John Knox, 1990).

Prothero, Stephen, *God is Not One: The Eight Rival Religions that Run the World* (New York: HarperOne, 2010).

Robeck, Cecil M., Jr, *The Azusa Street Mission and Revival: The Birth of the Global Pentecostal Movement* (Nashville: Thomas Nelson, 2006).

Robins, R.G., *A.J. Tomlinson: Plainfolk Modernist* (Oxford: Oxford University Press, 2004).

Runyon, Theodore. 'A New Look at "Experience"', *Drew Gateway* 57 (1988), pp. 44-55.

—(ed.), *Wesleyan Theology Today: A Bicentennial Theological Consultation* (Nashville: Kingswood, 1985).

—*The New Creation: John Wesley's Theology Today* (Nashville: Abingdon, 1998).

Saliers, Don E., 'Liturgy and Ethics: Some New Beginnings', *Journal of Religious Ethics* 7 (1979), pp. 173-89.

Scheick, William J., *The Writings of Jonathan Edwards* (College Station: Texas A & M University Press, 1975).

Shuman, Joel, 'Pentecost and the End of Patriotism: A Call for the Restoration of Pacifism among Pentecostal Christians', *Journal of Pentecostal Theology* 9 (1996), pp. 70-96.

Smith, James K.A., *Desiring the Kingdom: Worship, Worldview, and Cultural Formation* (Grand Rapids: Baker Academic, 2009).

—*Thinking in Tongues: Pentecostal Contributions to Christian Philosophy* (Grand Rapids: Eerdmans, 2010).

Solivan, Samuel, 'Orthopathos: Interlocutor between Orthodoxy and Praxis', *Andover Newton Review* 1 (1990), pp. 19-25.

—*The Spirit, Pathos and Liberation: Toward an Hispanic Pentecostal Theology* (JPTSup 14; Sheffield: Sheffield Academic Press, 1998).

Steele, Richard B., *'Gracious Affection' and 'True Virtue' according to Jonathan Edwards and John Wesley* (Metuchen: Scarecrow, 1994).

—(ed.), *'Heart Religion' in the Methodist Tradition and Related Movements* (Lanham: Scarecrow, 2001).

Stoffer, Dale R. (ed.), *The Lord's Supper: Believers' Church Perspectives* (Scottdale: Herald Press, 1997).

Strong, Douglas M., 'Sanctified Eccentricity: Continuing Relevance of the Nineteenth-Century Holiness Paradigm', *Wesleyan Theological Journal* 35 (2000), pp. 9-21.

Synan, H. Vinson, *The Holiness-Pentecostal Tradition: Charismatic Movements in the Twentieth Century* (Grand Rapids: Eerdmans, 1997).

Taylor, Charles, *Modern Social Imaginaries* (Durham: Duke University Press, 2004).

Thomas, John Christopher, *Footwashing in John 13 and the Johannine Community* (JSNTS 61; Sheffield: JSOT Press, 1991).

—'Footwashing within the Context of the Lord's Supper', in Dale R. Stoffer (ed.), *The Lord's Supper: Believers' Church Perspectives* (Scottdale: Herald Press, 1997), pp. 169-84.

—'Footwashing', *White Wing Messenger* 78 (November 2000), pp. 10-13.

Vanhoozer, Kevin J., *The Drama of Doctrine: A Canonical Linguistic Approach to Christian Theology* (Louisville: Westminster John Knox, 2005).

Vanier, Jean, *Drawn into the Mystery of Jesus through the Gospel of John* (New York: Paulist Press, 2004).

Volf, Miroslav and Dorothy C. Bass (eds.), *Practicing Theology: Beliefs and Practices in Christian Life* (Grand Rapids: Eerdmans, 2002).

Vondey, Wolfgang and Chris W. Green, 'Between This and That: Reality and Sacramentality in the Pentecostal Worldview', *Journal of Pentecostal Theology* 19 (2010), pp. 265-91.

Wacker, Grant, 'Review of *Vision of the Disinherited*', *Pneuma* 4 (1982), pp. 53-62.

—*Heaven Below: Early Pentecostals and American Culture* (Cambridge: Harvard University Press, 2001).

Wadell, Paul J., *Friendship and the Moral Life* (Notre Dame: University of Notre Dame Press, 1989).

Warrington, Keith, *Pentecostal Theology: A Theology of Encounter* (London: T & T Clark, 2008).

Webster, John, *Holiness* (Grand Rapids: Eerdmans, 2003).

Webster, John, Kathryn Tanner, and Iain Torrance (eds.), *The Oxford Handbook of Systematic Theology* (Oxford: Oxford University Press, 2007).

Welker, Michael (ed.), *The Work of the Spirit: Pneumatology and Pentecostalism* (Grand Rapids: Eerdmans, 2006).

Wells, Samuel, *Improvisation: The Drama of Christian Ethics* (Grand Rapids: Brazos, 2004).

Wesley, John, *The Letters of the Rev. John Wesley* (8 vols.; ed. John Telford; Epworth: London, 1931).

—*The Works of John Wesley, volumes 1-4* (ed. Albert C. Outler; Nashville: Abingdon, 1984-1987).

White, Charles Edward, *The Beauty of Holiness: Phoebe Palmer as Theologian, Revivalist, Feminist, and Humanitarian* (Eugene: Wipf and Stock, 2008).

Wilkinson, Michael and Steven M. Studebaker (eds.), *A Liberating Spirit: Pentecostals and Social Action in North America* (Eugene: Pickwick, 2010).

Wright, N.T., *The New Testament and the People of God* (Minneapolis: Fortress, 1992).

Yoder, John Howard, *The Politics of Jesus* (Grand Rapids: Eerdmans, 2nd edn, 1994).

—*The Christian Witness to the State* (Eugene: Wipf and Stock, 1998).

—*Discipleship as Political Responsibility* (Scottdale: Herald, 2003).

—*Christian Attitudes to War, Peace, and Revolution* (Grand Rapids: Brazos Press, 2009).

Yong, Amos, *Spirit-Word-Community: Theological Hermeneutics in Trinitarian Perspective* (Eugene: Wipf and Stock, 2002).

—*In the Days of Caesar: Pentecostalism and Political Theology* (Grand Rapids: Eerdmans, 2010).

Young, Frances, *The Art of Performance: Towards a Theology of Holy Scripture* (London: Darton, Longman and Todd, 1990).

Index of Biblical References

Index of Names

9 781935 931287